Sent Free

Sent Free

Mission and Unity
in the Perspective
of the Kingdom

Emilio Castro

World Council of Churches, Geneva

Cover design: Michael Dominguez
ISBN 2-8254-0821-2
© 1985 World Council of Churches, 150 route de Ferney,
1211 Geneva 20, Switzerland
No. 23 in the Risk book series
Printed in Switzerland

To my wife
Gladys

Table of contents

Preface

What is the mission of the church? What goal must it have? What kind of programmes and priorities must the church adopt in the pursuit of that goal?

Such questions are by no means new. In fact they are as old as the church itself. But they have been asked more pointedly than ever before during the last few decades, and answered more variously — and at times more acrimoniously.

The answers have ranged from church growth and the evangelization of the world in our time to Christian presence and humanization.

The debate on mission has gone on within churches and between them. It has gone on at local and national levels and regionally and internationally as well. The debate has given rise to unfortunate controversies and unhappy divisions.

It is my conviction that the mission of the church is the mission of the kingdom of God. Within the perspective of the kingdom, I am persuaded that we are sent free to be signs of the kingdom, witnessing to its presence in our midst and awaiting its coming in the future.

That perspective is broad, and within it we have innumerable possibilities of serving the kingdom and the Servant King whose it is, participating in the announcing of it and manifesting it in our different situations.

The situations are indeed different, as I try to illustrate in the first chapter of the book. The churches face different choices as they make missionary decisions, and the choices differ from place to place and situation to situation. But the different choices need not lead to conflict or competition. They reflect the richness of the kingdom and that recognition can result in unity in mission.

I am conscious of the fact that "kingdom" is not an "inclusive" word. In a book entitled *Announcing the Reign of God — Evangelization and the Subversive Memory of Jesus*, Mortimer Arias has given the following explanation for his use of the term kingdom of God, and I agree entirely with him:

> The term "kingdom" is an unfortunate one in today's world:
> it is seriously questioned by many because of its monarchical

political connotations and its associations with patriarchal structures and language. It is a particularly sensitive expression for those who are challenging the implications of sexist language and trying to translate the scriptures in a way that expresses their faith in non-sexist language. "Reign of God" has been suggested as a better alternative, and it is already in circulation. In my original language — Spanish — we use the word *reino*, which includes the meanings of kingdom, reign, and realm. Because I speak another language, I do not pretend to understand all of the nuances of the English language nor would I attempt to solve this sensitive issue. I would like, however, to share in this concern and to express my solidarity with those who feel discriminated against or oppressed by language. I accept the fact, however, that "kingdom of God" has become a technical term in theology and religious language and a symbol so intimately related to Jesus' message that we cannot avoid it. I hope that our study of the meaning Jesus gave to this special term will show precisely that the reign of God puts under judgment not only old monarchies and patriarchal values but any system that denies God-given freedom and dignity to any human being.

This book is based on the first section of a dissertation I wrote, as part of the doctoral requirements, for the University of Lausanne. The title of the dissertation was *Freedom in Mission: the Perspective of the Kingdom of God.* * My thesis was precisely that mission, understood in the perspective of the kingdom of God, allows — even demands — total freedom to serve that kingdom, to participate in its announcement and in its manifestation. I submitted that a recognition of this Christian freedom could generate untapped resources of imagination and energies in the churches; it could save us from frustrating discussions around secondary issues and provide unity for the most diverse forms of the church missionary vocations in the service of Jesus, the Servant King.

In preparing the original manuscript for publication in the Risk series, it was necessary to shorten the original text, leave out a number of quotations, and eliminate most of the

---

* The dissertation has been published in full, and is available from the WCC Publications Office.

footnotes. For my ideas and convictions I am indebted to a large number of friends, and the book as it now stands makes little acknowledgement of it. May I use this opportunity to express my deep debt of gratitude to many of my colleagues and friends whose ideas I have made my own and whose positions, even when they were different from mine, have helped me in my own journey of faith.

I am particularly grateful to my wife Gladys whose unfailing sympathy and support meant so much to me when I was working on this project.

Montpellier, France
October 1984

EMILIO CASTRO

1. The situation

For several years an American missionary shared the gospel with the local animistic people in a West African country. He is a committed Christian with an evangelistic orientation. He is back in the United States now. His present mission, he says, is to give whatever help he can to families whose gas supply is cut, in the middle of winter, because they are not able to pay the gas bills.

Any assembly of the World Council of Churches is seen to cover the most diverse human concerns: from genetics to the problems of Afghanistan, from nuclear power to monastic life, from worship to the condemnation of racism. No wonder some people have commented ironically: "They seem to be the UN at prayer!"

How do Christians and churches find and define their missionary obedience? Do we have a set of canonical laws or a discipline book which prescribes our missionary tasks and responsibilities? What is the specific vocation of Christians and churches? What makes a church different from other human communities involved in the service of humankind?

These are vital questions for the churches everywhere. They are questions of life and death for Christians in many parts of the world. Churches and Christians trace their missionary vocation to Jesus' commandment "to make disciples of all nations, baptizing them in the name of the Father, the Son and of the Holy Spirit, teaching them to observe all that I have commanded you" (Matt. 28:18-20). But they are divided in their assessment of what needs to be done as *mission* in particular places and times. There are even critical voices which question the very relevance of world mission, especially the possibility of its implementation through cross-cultural missions.

Such differences and reservations are basically expressions of different missionary options and priorities. But they are generally taken as conflicting options and irreconcilable approaches. Is it not possible, however, that they are complementary and not contradictory?

They are complementary in the sense that each one of our priorities could, or should, become an entry point to the total mission of God's love. Our affirmation of freedom in mission refers specifically to the unlimited possibilities which churches and Christians have to join in the struggle of the kingdom of God.

Let us take a look at some of the situations in the world today where churches try to define their mission as they face diverse circumstances and respond to different challenges.

Latin America — the burden of history

Latin America is the so-called Christian continent. We have had almost five centuries of Christian presence and evangelization. The priest came with the soldiers, the church with the conquerors. The strange mixture of the cross and the sword led to the Christianization of Latin America. It is, perhaps, the best example of the total conversion of a continent to the Christian faith. Statistically speaking, more than ninety per cent of the people in Latin America would consider themselves Christian, most of them Roman Catholic. So, if our fundamental criteria were the planting of the church, the growth of the church and the baptism of all people, we could indeed be very pleased with the situation in Latin America.

But these have also been centuries of domination and exploitation, and of the oppression of the native, black, and poor populations of Latin America. Can we, in the circumstances, feel satisfied because almost everybody is Christian? With what yardstick of the kingdom do we measure the situation in Latin America?

Today we are acutely aware of this ambiguous and sinful situation. Through data provided by the social sciences on the relations of power in Latin American society, we now understand how the economy works against poor people. We cannot any longer plead ignorance; we know how people are oppressed, and how political and economic forces work against them.

We do not only know the facts. We also see the awakening of people. Themselves conscientized, the poor people expect the churches to take a clear stand. The poor are discovering that their plight is not a matter of fate or providence. It is not God's will. It is the consequence of relations of power, and the prevailing structures in society, and so the poor are now organizing themselves to challenge those structures. These very same poor people, who are aware of their predicament, are members of churches and faithful participants in the life of congregations. The people of Latin America are poor, and they are believers! How will the churches respond to a faith that refuses to accept poverty as ordained by God?

The churches in Latin America have gone through a great biblical renewal. Since the Second Vatican Council, the whole attitude of the Roman Catholic Church to the Bible has changed dramatically; today in almost every country in Latin America it cooperates with the United Bible Society in the publication and distribution of the Bible. Thousands of basic ecclesial communities meet to read the Bible, to pray, and to face practical questions. How do we work for God's justice, they ask? How do we change our situation?

The theology of liberation has developed, and it has promoted a historical reading of the Bible which seeks to recover the socio-political and economic context in which the Bible was written, and tries to come to grips with the biblical message in relation to the social, political, cultural and economic realities of our day.

The knowledge we have acquired of our past and our present, the growing historical awareness of the poor, the biblical renewal — all these have dramatically posed the question to Latin American churches: What is our Christian vocation? What is our Christian identity? If the kingdom of God has to do with God's will in all realms of life, searching questions inevitably pose themselves to the Christian church.

And the answer was heard all over the continent: We are the church of the powerless Christ who made his own the fate of the poor and the least. Nothing short of the affirmation of *God's preferential option for the poor* and a programme evolved in the light of that affirmation can do justice to our present missionary calling.

In 1968 in Medellin, Colombia, and in 1979 in Puebla, Mexico, the Conference of Roman Catholic Bishops affirmed such solidarity with the poor. The pronouncements of both gatherings were preceded and followed by intense controversy. Traditionalists and progressivists clashed. Ideological differences were evident all along. But a clear emphasis has emerged. Within the Catholic Church there is a radical change of priorities and of pastoral emphases. Now it is in the middle of the turmoil produced in the social, political and economic life of these nations through this radical change. The alliance with the sword has given place to solidarity with the downtrodden and confrontation with the powerful.

So much for the four or five hundred years of Christian *Catholic* presence in Latin America. The Protestants came to Latin America in the second half of the nineteenth century. Most of them came invited by the more liberal-minded people, Free Masons, who were interested in fighting the cultural and political control of the Roman Catholic Church. Protestants could say: "We have rejected the traditional Christianity that is dominant in Latin America and we represent a more liberal outlook, a more progressive perspective."

But we must take such claims with a pinch of salt, because Protestantism brought its own neo-colonialism. The expansion of US Protestant churches abroad took place in a way that was suspiciously parallel to the colonial and commercial expansion of the United States. Thus, while it is true that simply because we are small in number we cannot, as Protestants, be accused of the same complicity that the Catholic Church had with the dominant establishment in Latin America, we cannot naively pretend to be innocent of the *de facto* complicity with the *actual* forces of domination in the life of our nations. Protestant missions also include new sects and groups, especially in Central America, which proclaim a gospel that defends the "values of western civilization". In the name of fighting communism, they work actively against all forces for change in Latin American society.

The Protestant churches, however, have gone through the same process of conversion as the Roman Catholic Church. They too have become aware of the situation of the poor and the socio-political forces behind poverty. This awareness came to be articulated institutionally at the conference in 1981, in Huampani, Peru, of the Latin American Council of Churches (CLAI) which represents more than a hundred Protestant churches. CLAI has taken a clear stand, and has called upon the churches to become involved in the struggle to overcome all dependence and oppression. "Wherever a single human being is prevented from living humanly, there we have a situation of sin. Love and justice must become manifest in all aspects of life."

Through a "Pastoral (ministry) of Consolation", CLAI has made the churches increasingly aware of the repeated violations of human rights, and of the plight of displaced populations and political refugees. For Protestant churches in Latin America, evangelism understood as church growth has been the non-negotiable priority. Now they are obliged to see that priority against the background of a new understanding of their past history and of the total human reality.

Our ecumenical challenge today, whether we are Catholic or Protestant, is to face the question: What is the missionary obedience that corresponds to our past history, does justice to our present awareness, and meets the demands of the kingdom, as we read the Bible today? In this ecumenical era we face together the question of the future.

Let me illustrate this with a few concrete situations.

Pope John Paul II visited Nicaragua in 1983. He spent only eight or nine hours in the country. He celebrated mass, when his message focused on the authority of the church.

The Pope wanted the Nicaraguan people, especially the Nicaraguan priests, to recognize the central authority of the bishops. He saw that the unity of the church was jeopardized by the participation of priests in the Sandinist government!

One particular episode during the visit dramatically illustrated the situation. On the Pope's arrival, Father Ernesto Cardenal, Minister for Culture, knelt before the Pope, who rebuked him and said: "You must put your relation with the church in order." In the Pope's understanding, the option of working at the political level, in this moment of the country's history, was the wrong option for a priest.

Of course, this could be interpreted simply as a political or ideological difference of opinion. The Pope and his advisers do not feel convinced that the Sandinist government can deliver the goods; the priests think it can. That is a matter of political judgment. But the discussion is not at that level, it relates to what is the *central* vocation or *priority* of the church.

What are the arguments for priests to go beyond the traditional observance of priestly functions in local parishes and assume responsibilities in the government of a nation? The Pope seems to be saying: "The kingdom of God must become manifest through the work of the parish." The priests are saying: "The kingdom of God must also become manifest through the building up of a new social organization in our country."

Or take a similar dilemma, now from a Protestant situation. In 1981, a military coup took place in Guatemala and a new general, Efraim Rios Montt, came to power. He announced that he was a "born again" Christian who belonged to a small church, Verbo, from California, USA. He supported a whole range of Protestant activities in the country. Several groups in the United States put to young people the challenge of a missionary vocation; their goal was to send one thousand American missionaries to Guatemala to take advantage of this God-given chance to evangelize a country with four or five hundred years of Christian history! While many new missionaries were going to Guatemala, and many evangelistic campaigns were under way, the genocide of the Indians in the mountains continued and those who were calling for justice continued to be eliminated.

For some Christians the kingdom of God in Guatemala demanded the defiance of the powerful; they opted to suffer with the little ones, even at the risk of death. For others the priority was to "save" as many souls as possible. Behind this dilemma is the same old question: What is the goal of Christian mission? Are we in the business of saving individuals who will receive a passport to go to certain bliss in heaven or are we called to announce the rule of God, calling for justice and the defence of the "little ones"? Are we in the business of "converting" individuals or are we called as

Christians to serve the cause of the kingdom of God which
involves the transformation of the whole reality?

Or are we posing the wrong questions? Do we need to accept this either/or? What is the interplay between a
religious experience and Christian participation in the total
human struggle?

Asia — a variety of options

Church growth and social justice

In South Korea, traditionally a Buddhist country, the
church is growing very fast. Today about twenty-two or
twenty-three per cent of the population confess the Christian faith. Church growth in Korea is a recent phenomenon,
and the rate of growth shows no sign of slowing down. But
the central concern of the churches there is not evangelism.
Evangelism simply happens!

The military government is interested in promoting and
supporting church work insofar as it gives the masses of
people a sense of achievement, and of success and hap-
piness. Through belonging to successful church movements,
people could become alienated from the problems of a
society that is growing too fast economically along neo-
capitalist lines. Christians are confronted with the question:
Should we be satisfied with growth at this pace, making it
our only goal, or should we also face the situation of the
little ones, the poor people, who are the victims of minimal
salaries and demanding work schedules, and are sacrificed
to promote the economic development of the society?

On the one hand, there are successful stories of church
growth and, on the other, stories of persons related to urban
industrial mission who are paying the price for organizing
the poor to struggle for their rights. But church growth and
social justice concerns do not contradict each other. Some
of those who go to jail are pastors of growing congregations!

Church growth is a very useful social tool; it makes the
churches all the more useful as they live in solidarity with
the poor. We cannot say no to evangelism and to church
growth because all people have the right to a personal

knowledge of Jesus Christ. Who am I to decide who should be converted and who should not?

No, theologically there is no contradiction. But here is a situation where we are confronted with the temptation to be content with the fact of rapid church growth and to sidestep questions of where the kingdom of God is suffering violence.

For the churches in Korea the challenge is to put all the gifts of the church, including its growth, at the service of the poor. It is to see the growth of the churches not as a process which takes people away from the real dilemmas of society, but as an invitation to participate in the total endeavour to shape society more in accordance with God's will and the pattern of God's kingdom.

Conversion or renewal?

With the single exception of the Philippines, Christianity in Asia is a minority religion, and it lives side by side with highly developed religious systems. It could be said that from a purely numerical point of view Christian mission in Asia has been a failure! But, important as numbers are, they do not tell the whole story. The kingdom values have been shared and the gospel has had its impact on Asian cultures.

We must, however, face the reality of missionary history. We cannot ignore the widespread revival of ancient religions. Nor can we ignore the need to work for a possibility of decent life for the masses of poor people in the Asian countries. No wonder Christians and churches are raising crucial questions, and rethinking the nature and the future of the missionary endeavour.

C.S. Song, a theologian from Taiwan, writes about the calling of Christians and churches to participate in the renewal and the re-animation of Asian cultures. They should not be ambassadors of western cultures. They are called to share the gospel from within the Asian cultures, participate fully in the renewal of the cultural life of the Asian nations — even in the renewal and re-animation of Asian religions.[1]

---

[1] *Christian Mission in Reconstruction*, Maryknoll, NY, Orbis, 1977.

Theologians in India have been working with similar realities. Should we baptize people into the Christian community? Often baptism symbolizes the breaking of family and communal ties; so should the "converts" be urged to remain in their families and communities, and try to discover the meaning of Christ from within the cultural and religious values of the nation? Is there any chance that a marriage similar to the one between the gospel and the Hellenistic culture could happen between the Indian culture shaped by religion and the Christian gospel? M.M. Thomas thus talks about a Christ-centred syncretism![2]

Tissa Balasuriya, a Roman Catholic theologian from Sri Lanka, expresses this passionate search for Asian Christian authenticity: "As an Asian I cannot accept as divine and true any teaching which begins with the presupposition that all my ancestors for innumerable generations are eternally damned by God unless they had been baptized in or were related to one of the Christian institutional churches. Theology must honestly respect these millions upon millions of my ancestors and future human beings, before I can accept theology as a true interpretation of revelation from a loving God, Father of all." And again: "We have to rethink basically our 'conversion mentality'. We have to rid ourselves of a competitive mentality with regard to other religions; suspicions need to be replaced by warmth and a desire for understanding."[3]

In January 1979 the Asian Theological Conference met in Sri Lanka around the theme "Asia's Struggle for Full Humanity: Towards a Relevant Theology". There conflict and tension surfaced as new and old perspectives clashed. With much difficulty the conference agreed upon a final statement. It said:

> To be authentically Asian, theology must be immersed in our historical-cultural situation and grow out of it. A theology that emerged from the people's struggle for liberation would spontaneously formulate itself in the religio-cultural idioms of the people.

---

[2] *Breaking Barriers*, ed. David M. Paton, Geneva, WCC, 1976, p.236.
[3] *Liberation of Theology in Asia*, Maryknoll, NY, Orbis, 1980, pp.19-20.

> In many parts of Asia, we must integrate into our theology the insights and values of the major religions, but this integration must take place at the level of action and commitment to the people's struggle.[4]

To some Christians outside Asia, all this will sound like dangerous language. We must listen, however, to what Christian people who are in daily contact with people of other religious persuasions are saying. They invite us to enter into a necessary dialogue with people of other faiths, and not to assume that a western, aggressive understanding of the missionary activity of the church is the only understanding that could be faithful to the gospel. We need to raise with them basic questions. For example, what are the kingdom values that one promotes when calling the Christian communities in Asia to participate in the renewal of society? What are the biblical criteria that are basic to one's option there? We could have different ways of expressing our Christian obedience but we need to be able to justify these to each other in terms of a basic common Christian conviction that is articulated in a way that will provide mutual inspiration and correction.

Africa — search for authenticity

Where is the Christian missionary priority at this given moment in Africa? Let me quote Desmond Tutu, the General Secretary of the South African Council of Churches. Writing about Christian churches and Christian theology in Africa, he says:

> African theology has failed to produce a sufficiently sharp cutting edge. It has seemed to advocate disengagement from the hectic business of life because very little has been offered that is pertinent, say, about the theology of power in the face of the epidemics of coups and military rule, about development, poverty, disease, and other equally urgent present-day issues. I believe this is where the abrasive black theology from America may have a few lessons for African theology. It may help to recall African theology to its vocation to be concerned for the poor and the oppressed, about (people's) needs for liberation

---

[4]*Ibid*, p.157.

from all kinds of bondage to enter into an authentic personhood which is constantly undermined by pathological religiosity and by political authority that has whittled away much personal freedom without too much opposition from the church.[5]

Look at his list of priorities of missionary options for the church: a consideration of the question of power from the Christian perspective, in the face of all the military coups that take place in Africa; a clear position on poverty, disease; the liberation from all kinds of bondage. Desmond Tutu is a bishop of the Anglican Church. Of course he is interested in all aspects of the life of the church, but he affirms that in the particular situation of South Africa or Africa in general they cannot go on with business as usual. They cannot be uninvolved; they are obliged to confront all these missionary frontiers where Christian presence and witness is necessary.

Many Christians in Africa are with Bishop Tutu in his passionate plea for Christian participation in liberation struggles. On this they are one with Christians from all regions of the world who realize the historical nature of the Christian gospel and the challenge to God's loving will posed by prevailing injustices. But African churches and African theologians do face specific problems and they are raising concrete theological questions. Fundamentally they are trying to recover an African identity, a sense of authenticity in their response to the gospel. They do this by affirming the values of the traditional culture and religions of Africa, not simply as a way to facilitate the penetration of the gospel, but to contribute to the total spiritual richness of the Christian church. So M. Oduyoye:

> We must note that since "traditional" life was permeated in all its aspects by religion, any appeal we make to traditional values and practices is ultimately religious. Also we must bear in mind that the basic element in religion does not consist of practices of cultic places and persons but the beliefs that are manifested through them. So that even when modernization has modified ceremonies and other cultic practices, human beings

---

[5]Quoted in *African Theology en Route*, Maryknoll, NY, Orbis, 1979, p.182.

12

will continue to depend on the beliefs as a rock on which to build. So, for example, the belief in the living-dead, in the existence of spirits, and in magic and witchcraft are a part of the African's recognition that life is not entirely materialistic. These beliefs are an expression of the yearning for life after life. Since the Supreme Being is believed to be the Source of Life, the search after the life-force is itself a groping for closer and more personal relationship with Being Itself.

To contribute more effectively to the religious development of people, African Christian theologians have a duty to theologize from this context and incorporate the authentic African idiom to Christian theology. Utilizing African religious beliefs in Christian theology is not an attempt to assist Christianity to capture and domesticate the African spirit; rather it is an attempt to ensure that the African spirit revolutionizes Christianity to the benefit of all who adhere to it.[6]

They also explore the many links existing between the biblical story and Africa.

Professor Kwesi A. Dickson elaborates on the continuity between the Old Testament and African life and thought.[7] Everywhere in Africa preachers point to the Exodus story, to the Queen of Sheba and King Solomon, and very specially to the refuge provided by Egypt to the infant Jesus and his parents. African independent churches emphasize this linkage as an affirmation of their belonging to the biblical tradition without any western mediation. Perhaps the most important illustration of this search for roots and identity is provided by the "Confession of Alexandria", drafted by the General Committee of the All Africa Conference of Churches in Cairo in 1976.

We have become conscious of the fact that we are inheritors of a rich tradition. Our current concern with issues related to economic justice, the total liberation of men and women from every form of oppression and exploitation, and peace in Africa, as well as our contemporary search for authentic responses to Christ as Lord over the whole of our lives has led us to a deeper understanding of the heritage delivered to us by the Fathers of the early church in North Africa. ... It is this heritage which'

---

[6]*Ibid.*, p.116.
[7]*Ibid.*, pp.95-107.

inspires us to confess that it is the same incarnate Christ who is calling us to respond to him in terms that are authentic, faithful and relevant to the men and women in Africa today.[8]

We must also remember that the missiological debate about moratorium developed in Africa, first through Dr John Gatu from Kenya, and later in the 1974 Assembly of the AACC. "The call to moratorium enabled Africans to ask if it was God's design to make their continent a mission field for Europeans and people of European descent. The moratorium closes the door on ideas tested elsewhere and opens the way for God's self-disclosure to people of every nation, race and tribe, and the development of programmes tuned to the real needs of people."

The fears and anxieties provoked by the debate on moratorium should not blind us to the central intention of the proposal, to open a space, an area of freedom, for the African churches where they could discover their own identity.

The older churches

The examples we have given from Africa, Asia and Latin America illustrate the diversity of the missionary dilemmas confronting the churches today. But because these examples are about the experience of what were called "younger churches" and relate to areas that the churches in Europe and America have considered as "mission fields", we are likely to be misunderstood.

We take for granted mission in six continents. We affirm that the very being of the church is missionary and that everywhere churches are sent to proclaim God's salvation to all people and to all areas of life. Very old churches are also confronted with old and new problems. The affirmation of freedom as the central missiological principle, and the vision of the kingdom as the frame and aim of Christian mission should provide for them also fresh possibilities to affirm their vocation and their faithfulness.

Take, for example, the Orthodox churches in northern Africa or the Middle East, surrounded by powerful Islamic communities which control the political power of their

---

[8] Nairobi, AACC, 1981.

nations — like Iran, Syria, Irak, Lebanon and Egypt. For over one thousand years they have not been allowed to develop any evangelistic work. Conversion to Christianity was legally prohibited and any attempt to convert people was discouraged — even invited punishment. They can only pass on faith from parents to children, generation after generation. They thus developed an understanding of the Christian mission that is not so much geographical or in terms of the expansion of the church, but chronological and sacramental.

Are the preservation of the church for the coming generations and the priestly intercessory prayer for the whole community "mission" in the model of Abraham? Is this concentration on the chronological and sacerdotal vocation a betrayal of the missionary command of the gospel or the faithful and relevant expression of it under peculiar circumstances?

Today these churches are facing a new situation. Many of their members have migrated to other continents and established churches there which serve their ethnic groups. The great challenge for them is to discover their new missionary potential in situations where the historical constraints are no more operative. The whole issue of the mission of the Orthodox diaspora demands ecumenical consideration.

In western Europe, we are passing from the situation of a "people's church" (Volkskirche), where everybody was supposed to belong to the church, to a very rapid de-Christianization process, at least a "de-churchification" process. Erstwhile majority churches are now obliged to rethink their mission in the light of new circumstances which have made them minorities in society.

What should be the mission of the faithful remnant in such situations? In the last two centuries it was very easy to equate mission with overseas mission. Now we not only talk about mission in six continents, we know that mission is at home, right in our neighbourhood.

W. Visser 't Hooft describes the situation in Europe as "neo-pagan".[9] Lesslie Newbigin traces the rise of the

---

[9] See *International Review of Mission*, Vol. LXVI, No. 264, 1977.

modern *Weltanschauung* and describes its failure to provide
an adequate frame of reference within which the contemporary challenges facing a technological society could be
tackled.[10] Both of them invite the churches to recover the
biblical message in living interplay with new historical situations.

In North America the churches continue to be full, but
more and more people are sceptical about "civil religion"
and question the easy identification of the American way of
life with the gospel of Jesus Christ. What is the relation
between church growth and faithfulness to the gospel,
between success and the cross of Jesus Christ?

The American churches send more missionaries abroad
than any other church. A passionate debate goes on in the
United Methodist Church between those who want to send
more missionaries — and more evangelistic-minded missionaries — and those who affirm the national leadership of
sister churches and the obligation to assume a political ad-
vocacy role on behalf of the third world. The debate is by no
means limited to the United Methodist Church. It raises
fundamental questions concerning our missionary
priorities.

Eastern Europe faces its own missionary challenges.
Here political, ideological and cultural life is organized
around the Communist Party. The churches which were
traditionally the focus of culture and national identity
have now — officially — been marginalized. In such circumstances the churches must look for different
theological perspectives and missiological options. J.
Hromadka and his theology of diakonia continue to in-
fluence churches in Czechoslovakia and Hungary. The
search for the people and the expression of the national
soul seem to be the response of the Roman Catholic
Church in Poland and of the Orthodox churches in
Bulgaria, Romania and the Soviet Union. Personal
evangelization, without any reference to or concern for
the social system, seems to be the answer of the
Pentecostal and free churches.

---

[10] *The Other Side of 1984*, Geneva, WCC, 1983.

New theologies: different departments

The churches in our day do indeed face a variety of missionary options. These options often give rise to controversy and conflict. They have also inspired a number of different theological systems and organizational schemes.

Even a few decades ago, the North Atlantic churches were the arbiters of Christian theology. Today the situation is totally different. Feminist theology, black theology, liberation theology, dialogue theology, minjung or people's theology — each one of these theologies attempts to see the missionary vocation of the church in a particular setting. They are basically missiologies. They are not explanations of God's being but represent a passionate search for new options for the mission of the churches.

Behind each of those theologies — liberation, African, black, feminist, minjung — there is a situation of conflict. No new theological system has emerged in the last twenty years that does not condemn some kind of oppression and affirm some specific perspective of the gospel which emerges out of the problems faced by the groups doing the theological work. In fact, most of these theologians say that their theology is an elaboration, *a posteriori*, of a stand taken in conflict situations. They are trying to explain themselves as Christians and to find guidelines for action.

These theologies also reflect the richness of the church in our day, the interplay of culturally linked manifestations of the Christian faith. We must try to understand how far these theological attempts represent responsible uses of our missionary freedom.

The programmatic division of labour within the structure of our churches illustrates another dimension of this problem. We have, in most of our western churches, departments for social action and departments for evangelism, each trying to be faithful to their particular mandate. This is useful up to a point, but it could also lead to an abdication of our total Christian responsibility. There are indeed different gifts in the life of the church. They call for a logical division of callings and of tasks. But if these charismas — whether considered individually or organized structurally in the life of the church — limit or distort the total witness to the kingdom, then they become a stumbling block for the mission of the church.

The problem becomes serious when the organizations created in western churches to relate to churches in the third world evolve bylaws and guidelines external to the churches themselves. For example, the fact that one can get substantial help for whatever goes under the magic term "development" but that it is much more difficult to get help for church growth, theological education, evangelism, etc., points to a sad distortion.

That a church or council of churches in a given country in Africa or Asia devotes the major part of its energies in the area of development does not necessarily mean that Christian people there are all convinced that it is through development that they must witness to the kingdom at this particular moment. It simply means that foreign funds are available for that particular work and are not available for other kinds of work. The question being asked is: How can each one of our particular concerns or gifts become an entry point to the total dynamic of the kingdom and not become departmentally isolated and stratified?

The kingdom and its freedom

Two fears haunt theologians. One is the fear of being unfaithful to the demands of today's world, the fear of being irrelevant, the fear of being out of touch. In the sixties in ecumenical discussions it was often heard that the "world must set the agenda". The church was thought of as responding to the priorities set in the world's agenda. The church is indeed sent into the world to respond to situations where human beings suffer, hope, live and die. But that does not mean that it has no mission of its own except to respond; no internal compulsion, no given convictions, no values that it must share with the world.

The other fear is that through being busy over the affairs of the world Christians might forget their essential vocation of proclaiming the gospel. It is the fear that in responding to the need to fight oppression, racism, sexism and similar evils, we might neglect our calling to "preach the word". If the proclamation of the gospel of the kingdom were possible without reference to the concrete human situations of the kingdoms in which we live, then of course our problem would be easy to solve! But the gospel happens in the encounter between the word of God and human beings living in specific situations.

It is our basic conviction that the kingdom of God is the central biblical category which gives content and direction to our missionary vocation. Our goal is the kingdom. The church is called to serve the kingdom, to be a privileged instrument of that kingdom, called in fact to exist for the sake of the kingdom.

We follow the living Christ, led by the Holy Spirit. Within the horizon of the kingdom of God, we have total freedom and total responsibility — a total freedom to discern, to plan and to act.

Given the nature of the kingdom, the liberty of the Spirit, the churches are free to respond to that freedom of God. Nothing can be *a priori* proscribed, among the action possibilities of the church. We refer to the freedom of the Spirit, calling Christians to different responses. We call this presence of the risen Christ and this action of the Holy Spirit missionary freedom, because it invites us to respond and persuades us to act. We could substitute "responsibility" for freedom, but I rather prefer the word freedom because it opens up our imagination and provides much more space than the word responsibility. It is, however, by being free that we are able to act responsibly.

We shall look to the ministry of Jesus and to the history of the early church to find there examples of freedom that could serve as inspiration and provide guidelines for our own situation.

When we use the word freedom theologically we mean the gift of the Holy Spirit that enables us to respond; but we need to look at that freedom possibility in sociological and political terms as well. I could claim that I am freed, but in fact I might be a victim of my own biases, social prejudices and class advantages. As when the rich white people in South Africa find support for apartheid in the Bible and claim that they are using their Christian freedom!

After the great teachers of suspicion — Marx, Freud and Nietzsche — we are only too aware of the constraints that work against real freedom. We cannot ingore those constraints even in the life of the church. But the Bible, the findings of human scientific disciplines, the community of faith, especially in its ecumenical dimensions, and the praxis of love — all provide reference points that will help us, if not to escape from these historical constraints, at least to struggle to transform them in the perspective of the coming kingdom.

2. The debate

Bangkok 1973

Through a series of international encounters we have in our century pursued the search for missionary clarity. Edinburgh 1910, to which we trace the beginnings of the modern ecumenical movement, was the first in the series. It was followed by several periodic meetings. The world mission conference convened by the Commission on World Mission and Evangelism of the World Council of Churches was the eighth in the series. It met in Bangkok.

There were, however, significant differences between the Edinburgh and Bangkok meetings. In 1910, the participants represented western Protestant missionary agencies. There were only a handful of participants from the "younger churches". At Bangkok, the majority of delegates came from the younger churches; there were delegates from Orthodox churches, and a fraternal delegation from the Roman Catholic Church.

There were also differences in content. Edinburgh had agreed not to consider "doctrinal" matters — to avoid polemics. Bangkok is perhaps the first missionary conference to take for its theme a central faith affirmation: "Salvation Today". In general, missionary gatherings discuss how to reach people and how to develop the missionary task; they are concerned with methodologies, approaches and practices. Bangkok focused rather on the salvation we are proclaiming. It addressed itself to the question: What is the meaning today of the central affirmation of our Christian faith that there is salvation in Jesus Christ?

In preparation for the conference, a fascinating book on the theme was published with stories from many parts of the world, dealing with the actual experience of salvation. The stories explored the relationship of salvation to diverse areas of life.[1] Bangkok examined the heart of our conviction that God is a saving God, and asked how this conviction could come alive and become real in the missionary task of the church.

Bangkok is the capital of Thailand, a Buddhist country where only one out of a thousand people is Christian. The

---

[1] *Salvation Today and Contemporary Experience*, Geneva, WCC, 1972.

location influenced the conference at two very different levels. First, the whole question of Christian attitude towards other religions — in this situation Buddhism — inevitably came up for discussion. Two attitudes were evident at the assembly. One of them was expressed by the General Secretary of the Church of Christ in Thailand, who preached the opening sermon on Isaiah 53 and Romans 5. He emphasized salvation by grace through faith in Christ. He explained that the main concern of the Church of Christ in Thailand was church growth; the goal was to double the membership of the church in four years. So they preached to people and invited them to become Christians and to join the church.

Another attitude towards Buddhism surfaced when a few Buddhist monks attended a plenary session. A dialogue took place between religious leaders in Thailand and a selected group of assembly delegates. It illustrated an approach that pointed to the need to respect other religions and to learn from them.

The official report of the conference makes only a passing reference to this encounter with Buddhists. But the exposure to a Buddhist culture and the experience of a minority church left a lasting impression upon all participants. It is significant that an ecumenical consultation was organized in Chiang Mai, Thailand, four years later, to discuss the whole issue of dialogue with different faiths. That encounter resulted in a document called "Guidelines for Dialogue with People of Living Faiths and Ideologies", where the witnessing and listening dimensions of Christian mission are brought together.

When the delegates at Bangkok talked about salvation, they were well aware that they were surrounded by millions of people who too were seeking salvation, though their lives were centred in a totally different set of values. The challenge of other religions remains an open question in the missionary task of the church. What is the place of other religions in God's kingdom?

The second important consequence of meeting in Thailand was that the delegates were made acutely aware of American military presence. From an American air base in the neighbourhood bombers were taking off at regular intervals to deliver their lethal load over the city of Hanoi and its surroundings. A delegate from the Netherlands proposed that we go to Hanoi and demonstrate our solidarity with the people. It was a dramatic moment. The international press promptly reported that a conference of Christians wanted to go to Hanoi. We did not go to Hanoi, but the word salvation took on a new meaning. And it helped us to understand the passion, the tensions, that pervaded the conference. Here we were, Christians, talking about salvation, while twenty miles away the messenger of death was taking off to kill and destroy. It was impossible to speak of salvation without relating it to this historical reality. History, the political reality, was very much present in the minds of the delegates; they were forced to consider the relation of salvation to the world events of the day.

Bangkok described salvation in terms that indicated its global, holistic nature. Salvation is seen at work in the struggle for economic justice and for human dignity, in the struggle against the alienation of person from person; and in the struggle of hope against despair in personal life. "The salvation which Christ brought, and in which we participate, offers a comprehensive wholeness in this divided life. We understand salvation as newness of life — the unfolding of true humanity in the fullness of God (Col. 2:9-10). It is salvation of the soul and the body, of the individual and society, humankind and the 'groaning creation'" (Rom. 8:19).[2]

The salvation Christ brings offers comprehensive wholeness, and this wholeness is newness of life. It is true humanity, the salvation of the total person's soul and body — and person means individual and society. The salvation of humankind embraces the whole of creation. This global and holistic understanding of salvation was accompanied by a recognition that we cannot always be totally inclusive. We have a global understanding of salvation that has to do with all aspects of the person, with all aspects of the person's relation to society, with all aspects of humankind's relation to nature. But we cannot always be totally inclusive. We are obliged to enter into this total salvation through particular doors.

---

[2]*Bangkok Assembly, 1973*, Geneva, WCC, p.88.

There are historical priorities according to which salvation is anticipated in one dimension first, be it the personal, the political, or the economic dimension. This point of entry differs from situation to situation in which we work and suffer. We should know that such anticipations, such entry points, are not the whole of salvation, and we must keep in mind the other dimensions while we work. Forgetting this denies the wholeness of salvation. Nobody can do in any particular situation everything at the same time. There are various gifts and tasks, but there is one Spirit and one goal.[3]

There are certain priorities, and we must use our freedom to discern them. There are various gifts and tasks — personal gifts, personal tasks, personal vocations — but there is one Spirit and one goal. And now comes the most polemic phrase in the report of the conference. "In this sense" — this sense of historical priorities, anticipations — "it can be said, for example, that salvation is the peace of the people in Vietnam, independence in Angola, justice and reconciliation in Northern Ireland, and release from the captivity of power in the North Atlantic community, or personal conversion in the release of a submerged society into hope, or of new life-styles amidst corporate self-interest and lovelessness."[4]

There are historical priorities, dimensions, particular gifts which are entry points into the dynamic of the kingdom and the reality of salvation. In a given moment, the conference says, "peace in Vietnam is salvation". Those who are working for peace in Vietnam are fulfilling a missionary role. Those who are looking for reconciliation in Northern Ireland are also discharging a missionary duty. Those who are inviting people to conversion within societies which deprive people of their humanity are working for the kingdom. But each one of these are entry points, historical priorities, anticipations of salvation in response to one particular gift or in the pursuit of one particular goal.

This is central to our work in the formulation of historical or contextual priorities as points of entry into the total struggle of the kingdom of God. This part of the Bangkok

[3] *Ibid.*, p.90.
[4] *Ibid.*

statement was much misunderstood and widely misinter-
preted. People concentrated on the second part: "Salvation
is peace in Vietnam." Of course we cannot think of salvation apart from the aspect of reconciliation with God and
our neighbours, and life eternal. But the statement does not
say the *whole* of salvation is peace in Vietnam; it is only
commended as one historical priority. It is one dimension.
It is one anticipation. It is an entry point. We should not
forget the other dimensions that will complete the picture,
but we need to enter by a particular door if we want to be
concrete in our missionary obedience. Our freedom in mission is so that we may be relevant in mission.

This understanding should help reconcile certain Christian positions that seem contradictory. If peace in Vietnam
is the entry point into the kingdom or the missionary
priority for Christians concerned with that nation, could it
not be that building the church and calling to conversion
should also be recognized as an entry point and as the
aspect to be emphasized in certain other parts of Asia and
of the world?

The Bangkok assembly had heard of the "growing questioning among people in Bangkok about the meaninglessness of life for many, and their search for
something deeper, indeed for a new identity".[5] If there is
this meaninglessness, then sharing the story of the gospel
is indeed important in that situation. But even as the concern for peace in Vietnam is not the whole of salvation, so
also telling the story of Jesus is not the whole of salvation
unless in both cases we point with our words and our
deeds beyond those particular emphases, to the total
dynamics of the kingdom of God. The theological approach of Bangkok, while providing examples of priorities
in terms of political and social situations, did not fail to
recognize other priorities that have traditionally held sway,
like the preaching of the word and the building of the
church. We should see all of them as legitimate entry
points into the total mission of the church, and ingredients
in the total meaning of salvation.

[5] *Ibid.*, p.78.

Bangkok under attack

After Bangkok, the debate centred on the implications of statements like the ones we have quoted. Some of the evangelical friends saw in them a confirmation of certain emphases that they trace to the Uppsala Assembly of the World Council in 1968. They protested against the reduction of theology to a kind of anthropology and of Christian faith to a kind of humanism. Hal Lindsell, the former editor of *Christianity Today*, said that the emphasis in Uppsala that came to fruition in Bangkok was on "humanization, secularization, socio-political involvement, economic development of third world nations, the elimination of racism, revolution, and a virulent anti-American feeling that centred on the war in Vietnam. The gospel of personal salvation through the substitutionary atonement of Christ on Calvary was supplanted by a secularized this-worldly version of social action as the mission of the church."[6]

He was not the only one who interpreted Bangkok that way; persons more friendly to the World Council also offered similar criticism. Arthur Glasser from Fuller Theological Seminary said that in Bangkok "the cultural mandate was central rather than the evangelistic mandate". He said, describing the evangelistic and cultural mandates, that "salvation really has implications for both. According to the cultural mandate, God decides to involve men in accepting responsibility for the world. He is concerned about the poor, the oppressed, the weak. He is concerned about government, injustice, oppression, and so on." But, Glasser says, this is one dimension of the Christian calling. The other dimension, the evangelistic dimension, he does not see very clearly in Bangkok.[7]

Towards the end of the conference the official representative of the Vatican, Father Jerome Hamer, greeted the delegates on behalf of the Roman Catholic fraternal delegation. He said very frankly: "I am appalled that you people can discuss salvation today, day after day, in all of its

---

[6]See Ralph Winter, ed., *The Evangelical Response to Bangkok*, Pasadena, William Carey Library, 1973, p.125.
[7]*Ibid.*, pp.90-91.

ramifications, but not listen to what the apostle Paul said about it. I have not heard anyone speak of justification by faith. I have not heard anyone speaking of everlasting life. What about God's righteous wrath against sin?"

We must also note the criticism that came from the Russian Orthodox Church, voiced in a letter addressed to the WCC Central Committee Moderator, M.M. Thomas from India. It expressed "perplexity and great regret" that there was no significant reference to eternal life in the letter sent to churches from Bangkok. That letter seemed to project "a one-sided and detrimental understanding of salvation in the spirit of boundless horizontalism" and had little to say on moral perfection here and eternal life hereafter.

Values at stake

These three critical responses — the evangelical, the Roman Catholic, and the Orthodox — each point to a value which needs to be cherished and preserved. Evangelicals and Roman Catholics ask for a more clear message addressed to individuals, in terms of their personal relation to God, their need for forgiveness and faith and their longing for eternal life. They could not hear in the heated debates in Bangkok this invitation to faith and personal conversion. The Russian Orthodox Church did not hear a clear reference to eternal life in God as the goal of all Christian expectation of salvation. Personal conversion, evangelism in terms of an invitation to a personal faith, eschatological hope in God — all these are central Christian affirmations which the people gathered in Bangkok would never deny. Their concern was to correct the deviations of the past and read the *kairos* of God, where the Spirit was calling the church to act obediently today.

Bangkok broke new ground; in some ways it was even talking a new language which was somewhat difficult to understand. What were the values at stake for the people gathered in Bangkok? They wanted to keep in mind the interplay, even the unity, between religious and secular history, between salvation history and human history. For Arthur Glasser, there is a cultural mandate and an evangelistic mandate; both are necessary, but they are different. Bangkok attempted to see the evangelistic dimension within the cultural mandate; and within the evangelistic dimension, the need to call for the recognition of the lordship of Christ over all cultures and kingdoms.

Thus in Bangkok, there was the attempt to take seriously the cultural history given to us, to root our church, our theology, the gospel, in the past of our nation, and, within that history, to participate in the liberation of our people and the building of our culture, in the creation of new human relations in an eschatological perspective — with the hope of contributing to the richness of the final banquet of the kingdom of God.

What Bangkok said is not very different, in fact, from what Orthodox theologians have been saying. Christians should become the ferment within history which could save that history. The transfiguration of the world is the goal towards which our Christian mission should work. The Holy Spirit is at work in the whole of creation. And that was what Bangkok attempted to express — to bring these theological affirmations down to earth and put them in the language of social, political and historical realities. We discerned in Bangkok that the theological schizophrenia that separates relations with God from relations with our neighbours disappears in the wonderful knowledge of a God whose Spirit works through different agents of liberation. Nor did we fail to recognize that God, fundamentally through the church, conveys to humankind the secret of divine love and offers the possibility of a conscious decision to incorporate our service in the divine mission of salvation and liberation.

This understanding of salvation redeems the historical task of humankind and provides the basis for all evangelistic work. Nothing human is foreign to the Christian community. In the birth of a child, in its development as a person, in the person's integration into the human community, in the fight for freedom of the whole community, in the search for more human forms of life — in all these we see the manifestation of God's care and love. The God who was active in the Exodus, providing freedom for the people of Israel, and the God who acted through the death and resurrection of Jesus Christ and offers new life to all humankind, is the same God who has called us to work for total human salvation.

The evangelical debate

A second important element in the discussion of mission has been the evangelical concentration on the evangelization of the world. A congress on world evangelism, called by the Billy Graham organization and the magazine *Christianity Today*, met in Berlin in 1966. It was followed in 1974 by a second congress, attended by 4,000 participants, in Lausanne, Switzerland, around the theme: "Let the Earth Hear His Voice". The Lausanne Covenant, although it was not an official document of the congress itself, was prepared and signed during that congress, is a good summary of the convictions of the Lausanne congress. According to it "more than 2,700 million people, which is more than two-thirds of humankind, had yet to be evangelized. We are ashamed that so many have been neglected. It is a standing rebuke to us and to the whole church." The congress coined the phrase "reaching the unreached" as the main slogan to mobilize the church.

While this slogan reflects the numerical and geographical dimension of the problem, the word "unreached" does not quite explain the situation. It seems to imply that there are people who have not been reached even by God, and that, of course, belongs to a dimension of reality that is hidden from us. God alone knows where and whom the Spirit has reached and in what form. This is not to deny the tragic fact that the vast majority of the population of the world has not embraced the Christian faith and that Christians are commanded to share the gospel of Jesus Christ with everybody, because it is God's will that everybody should come to the knowledge of the truth and be saved (1 Tim. 2:4).

Lausanne was not a response to Bangkok. The organizers of the congress did not think of it as such. Their concern was the evangelization of the world, understood as the telling of the story of Christ to people so that they might be converted; they were discussing the ways and means to reach that goal. Implicit in the discussions was a criticism of the World Council of Churches and the Commission on World Mission and Evangelism — which had concentrated on issues of culture and justice at a missionary conference! Unavoidably, however, most of the participants were affected by the same historical events as the delegates in Bangkok. They came from the same world at war; they were reading the same Bible; most of them came from the same churches. Sixty-five per cent of the 4,000 people in Lausanne were from member churches of the World Council of Churches. They too were trying to be faithful to the Holy Spirit. The result was that the Lausanne Covenant incorporated some of the key concepts of Bangkok — dialogue, moratorium, justice, culture — but tried to give those concepts a more precise definition in order to make sure that they did not obscure the basic tasks of the missionary vocation.

Distinctions are made; priorities established. Evangelism is defended as an independent category, related to but independent of the demands of social justice. "Social justice is not evangelization," it was said very clearly. But "...social justice belongs to our mandate". Bangkok raised moratorium as a possibility to stop the sending of missionaries and funds to a particular church, for a given period, to give that church a chance to discover its own self and to find its own identity in relation to the surrounding community. The Covenant indicates that moratorium, if it could liberate funds for other regions not yet reached by the gospel, might not be a bad idea! Dialogue is needed — provided it facilitates evangelization!

Lausanne marks the beginning of a coming together of different theological positions regarding the mission of the church.

Within the evangelical family, there has been a growing demand for an evangelical commitment to the reality of historical change, and to participation in human struggles for justice. In fact, in Lausanne itself a sizeable number of delegates had signed a complementary statement to the Covenant called "A Response to Lausanne". It is a more radical paper but it does not contradict the Covenant. It affirms the Covenant, but highlights the dimension of social justice and the need for social involvement by Christians.

A world consultation was organized by the Lausanne Committee for World Evangelization in June 1980 in Pattaya, Thailand. Its purpose was to study at greater depth the question of techniques and methodologies for reaching specific groups. The original intention was to confine the discussion to practical considerations of how to undertake the evangelization of Muslims, Hindus, nominal Catholics, nominal Protestants, and similar identifiable sections of people. But a number of participants, especially from the third world, under the leadership of Bishop David Gitari from Kenya, asked the organizing committee to include the consideration of questions of justice in the world and the responsibility of Christians in relation to such questions. They argued that the Lausanne Covenant recognized the importance of justice in relation to evangelism, and they were afraid that the Lausanne Committee for World Evangelization was now following a one-sided interpretation of the Covenant by keeping the concerns of evangelism unrelated to the total concern of God for the whole human situation. They wanted a world conference to be convened on the theme of Christian social responsibility to consider issues of justice, especially their relationship to evangelization. That gave rise to an internal debate within the committee. The fear was expressed, particularly by the church growth school in America, that such a conference could distort perspectives and betray the original vocation of the Lausanne movement. In the view of the church growth school, the Lausanne Committee should be concerned basically with the expansion and growth of the church, with reaching the unreached, while others could feel free to express their concern for social justice.

There have been efforts by other groups which are even more committed to the calling to reach the "unreached". For example, Ralph Winter from Pasadena, California (USA), would say that the real challenge today is to reach those who are beyond our cultural borders and that cannot be attempted at the level of local congregations. For such a task one needs more specialized organizations, as well as people who have a particular vocation, to cross cultural frontiers and evangelize people of other cultures.

This was the rationale behind a conference which was held in Edinburgh in 1980. The conference did not produce a covenant or a statement. It did, however, produce a pledge, which participants were urged to sign. It read:

"A Church for Every People by the Year 2000"
By the grace of God and for his glory
I commit my entire life
to obeying his commission of Matthew 28:18-20
wherever and however he leads me
giving priority to the peoples
currently beyond the reach of the gospel (Romans 15:20-21)
I will also endeavour to impart this vision to others.

There were strict doctrinal requirements for participation in this conference, which meant that its impact was limited to a small sector of the Christian community.

Meanwhile, an increasing number of evangelicals, especially from the third world, claimed that the concern for human justice had always belonged to their tradition. The best evangelists never made a clear-cut separation between the two. They might have made distinctions; they might have prescribed one direction for today and another for tomorrow, but they were convinced that the task of evangelism should point towards the total mission of God, including the concern for justice.

To respond to this concern and to face squarely the internal differences, two complementary meetings were called. The one organized by the Lausanne Committee for World Evangelization and the World Evangelical Fellowship brought 50 evangelical leaders to Grand Rapids, USA, in June 1982, to consider the relation between evangelism and social responsibility. "Many fear", they said, "that the more we evangelicals are committed to the one, the less we shall be committed to the other." The consultation affirmed that "evangelism and social responsibility, while distinct from one another, are integrally related in our proclamation of and obedience to the gospel. The partnership is in reality a marriage."[8]

---

[8] *Evangelism and Social Responsibility*, The Grand Rapids Report, Exeter, Paternoster Press, 1982, p.24.

The World Evangelical Fellowship organized in Wheaton, Illinois, in 1983 a series of three simultaneous consultations on "The Church in Local Settings", "The Church in New Frontiers of Mission", and "The Church in Response to Human Need". The concern for a clear relation between evangelism and social justice, voiced in Lausanne, raised in Pattaya, alive in communities like the Sojourners' community in the USA and in movements like the Fellowship of Evangelical Theologians in Latin America, was clearly articulated at these meetings:

> The reality of the presence of the kingdom gives us the courage to begin here and now to erect signs of the coming kingdom by working prayerfully and consistently for greater justice and peace and towards the transformation of individuals and societies. Since one day God will wipe away all tears, it grieves us to see people suffer now. Since one day there will be perfect peace, we are called to be peacemakers now. We humbly yet urgently call upon you, the churches, to stand with us in this ministry of practising love and seeking to restore the dignity of human beings created in the image of God.

There is an eschatological vision: the kingdom will bring the shalom (peace) of God, and God will wipe away our tears, bringing perfect peace, whole salvation. That vision urges us to be active in history, helping those who suffer now, working for peace, opposing all injustice. Because we are on our way to the kingdom, we are called to plant signs of the kingdom in this place and at this moment. We may well have theological differences, but we are convinced that God's calling to the church is a holistic calling. That is a living reality, and here we have a truly ecumenical meeting point.

Nor can we forget that the evangelical movement is primarily concerned with the evangelization of the whole world, especially of the millions of people who have not yet heard of Jesus Christ. We may or may not agree with some methodologies advocated; we may disagree with the understanding of people outside the Christian church as "lost". But the gospel needs to be shared. It cannot be the private property of Christians. We do not have the right to prevent anyone from coming to the knowledge of Jesus Christ. In this particular concern for individuals, there is a valid reminder of the question of faith in our world today. The missiological discussion in ecumenical circles, however, has been more concerned with the question of faithfulness in mission, of integrity, of the necessary correspondence between word and action; it recognizes that the lack of faithfulness on the part of Christian people is the main stumbling block in all evangelistic enterprises. Our evangelical friends have been more concerned with the actual attempt to provide an opportunity for people to come to faith in Christ. The two concerns belong inseparably together. Without a faithful community that in itself is a sign of the kingdom it will be difficult to convince the world of the radical newness of the gospel of Jesus Christ. But every attempt to be faithful involves the desire to share the gospel with others. Evangelism belongs to our faithfulness towards God. Without a commitment to evangelism our Christian commitment is incomplete. At the same time we need to bring together these dimensions of faithfulness and faith because becoming a Christian, being invited to accept Jesus Christ, means to be invited also to participate in his kingdom, in his own movement of love in history. By becoming Christians we cannot escape from history.

The Roman Catholic position

In 1974 a Synod of Bishops of the Roman Catholic Church took place in Rome around the theme "The Evangelization of the World". Synods of Bishops in the Catholic Church assist the Pope in his pastoral and teaching function. In general, they reflect the collective wisdom of the bishops; their findings are then shared with the Pope, who later incorporates them in whatever he wants to say on his own authority.

On 8 December 1975, the Pope published an apostolic exhortation under the title *Evangelii Nuntiandi* (Evangelization of the Modern World). He recognized the work of the bishops and then went on to elaborate on it. Paul VI began with the reminder that the presentation of the gospel message is not optional for the church. It is a duty laid on it by the command of the Lord Jesus so that people can believe and be saved. Christ is the supreme evangelist. He proclaims the kingdom and in the kingdom a liberating salvation; he accompanies his evangelistic mission with evangelical signs, and especially one sign to which Christ gives great importance — that the humble and the poor are evangelized. The disciples of John the Baptist asked Jesus: "Are you the one that we were expecting or do we need to wait for somebody else?" Jesus did not answer yes or no. He said: "Tell John what signs are being manifested — the healing of the sick, and the poor have good news preached to them" (Luke 7:18-23). The announcing of the gospel to the poor was one sign of the kingdom, a clear sign of the messianic vocation of Jesus. For the Pope, the task of evangelizing all people constituted the essential mission of the church.

In this he agreed with the General Secretary of the WCC, Dr Philip Potter, who, addressing the Synod, declared that "evangelization is the test of the ecumenical vocation". He also agreed with the Lausanne emphasis that evangelization is the central, essential mission. The church evangelizes when it "seeks to convert solely through the divine power of the message she proclaims both the personal and collective consciences of people, the activities in which they engage, and the lives and concrete milieu which are theirs".

There is a tension here. The Pope wants to make it clear that evangelization, in the sense of calling people to faith in Christ, is the central vocation of the church. At the same time, he recognizes that it is impossible to fulfill that mission without relating it to all aspects of people's lives.

The salvation that is promised by Christ is transcendent and eschatological, but it has its beginning in this life. Therefore the message is also "about the rights and duties of every human being, about family life, life in society, about international life, peace, justice, and development". It is "a message especially energetic today about liberation".

It is clear that the Pope wants to affirm two things — keeping them in creative tension. First, salvation has to do with eternal life; it is something that depends on our relation to God in Christ with consequences which go far beyond our daily historical life. At the same time, it also has consequences for human life here and now, and there "it is impossible to accept that in evangelization one could or should ignore the importance of the problems so much discussed today concerning justice, liberation, development and peace in the world. This would be to forget the lesson which comes to us from the gospel concerning love of our neighbour who is suffering and in need."

But the Pope says, talking about the church, that "she reaffirms the primacy of her spiritual vocation and refuses to replace the proclamation of the kingdom by the proclamation of forms of human liberation. She even states that her contribution to liberation is incomplete if she neglects to proclaim salvation in Jesus Christ." There would not be many people in the Catholic Church who would like it to replace the proclamation of the kingdom of God by the proclamation of human liberation of one kind or another. Many people would like, however, to see the manifestation of the kingdom of God in forms of human liberation as a pre-taste, as *avant-garde* of the kingdom. The Pope himself indicates that Christ carried out his proclamation through innumerable signs which amazed the crowds, and that the most important sign was that the poor were evangelized. So, words and deeds, signs and miracles, are all components of our proclamation, an anticipation and living out of the kingdom of God.

The Pope also recognizes the freedom we have to respond to the most diverse contexts. His concern is to make sure that our concern for liberation should not be conceived as taking the place of the announcement of salvation in Christ. It is the same concern expressed in the letter from the Russian Orthodox Church to the World Council of Churches which urged that we should not forget the eschatological nature of salvation and the reality of eternal life.

The positive side of the *Evangelii Nuntiandi* is its affirmation of the need to name the name of Christ — to point to him, his life, his teaching, his death, his resurrection — in our evangelization, and the simultaneous recognition that mission and evangelism involve responsibility for all realms of life. The dialogue on evangelism both within the Roman Catholic Church and in the ecumenical movement could profit from a new reading of "The Constitution of the Church in the Modern World" and from the work of theologians of liberation who attempt to overcome the dualism between eschatological salvation and historical liberation.

Is it possible to preserve this dimension of eternal life, the eschatological consummation of our salvation, and at the same time to see the operation of this salvation in our day-to-day history?

Nairobi 1975 — towards a convergence

In Nairobi, Kenya, in 1975, the Fifth Assembly of the World Council of Churches met around the theme "Jesus Christ Frees and Unites". One of the six sections concentrated on "Confessing Christ Today". This Assembly, and in particular this section, had the benefit of the participation of people who had been in Bangkok and in Lausanne, as well as Roman Catholic advisers. Nairobi, therefore, was the first ecumenical gathering that could attempt to bring together the different positions.

The Lausanne Covenant on World Evangelization, the Pope's encyclical and "Confessing Christ Today" — all of them wish to preserve a clear doctrinal content, the core of evangelization and, at the same time, make a serious commitment to the cause of human justice. Nairobi, responding to that concern, said: "The gospel always includes the announcement of God's kingdom and love through Jesus Christ, the offer of grace and forgiveness of sins, the invitation to repentance and faith in him, the summons to fellowship in God's church, the command to witness to God's saving words and deeds, the responsibility to participate in the struggle for justice and human dignity, the obligation to denounce all that hinders human wholeness and a commitment to risk life itself."[9]

---

[9]*Breaking Barriers: Nairobi 1975*, David M. Paton ed., Geneva, WCC, 1976, p.52. The quotations that follow are also from the same book.

Bangkok had affirmed the value of entry points; because we cannot do everything everywhere at every moment, we must, through particular obedience to one particular aspect of the gospel, enter into the whole of the gospel.

Nairobi affirmed that the gospel *always* includes "the participation in the struggle for justice, the obligation to denounce all that hinders human wholeness". Having learned from the critical responses to Bangkok, Nairobi used certain safeguards to avoid misunderstanding: "We regret that some reduce liberation from sin and evil to social and political dimensions, just as we regret that others limit liberation to the private and eternal dimensions." But participants were conscious of the fact that millions of people have not had a chance to hear the gospel, and in that awareness they confessed the failure of the churches to be faithful to their vocation to share the gospel with every creature.

Nairobi was a friendly Assembly. In a reconciling mood it reminded Christians that to be engaged in mission and evangelization meant a costly discipleship. "Confessing Christ and being converted to his discipleship belong inseparably together. Those who confess Jesus Christ deny themselves, their selfishness and slavery to the godless 'principalities and powers', take up their crosses and follow him." Then the Assembly spelt out the cost of discipleship, the price that many people are paying today for being faithful to the gospel. It deplored "cheap conversions, without consequences" and "a superficial gospel preaching, an empty gospel without a call into personal and communal discipleship".

Melbourne 1980 — the poor

In 1980 the Commission on World Mission and Evangelism of the World Council called another missionary conference, this time in Melbourne, Australia. The main theme was the prayer of Jesus, "Your Kingdom Come". The selection of the theme was in itself a spiritual exercise; it was an attempt to discern the situation of humankind today, in the light of the biblical message. There was the deep awareness of the seriousness of human suffering in the

world and the conviction that there were no ready-made
human solutions. The best thing, it was felt, would be to
concentrate on the prayer of Jesus. The increasing polariza-
tion in the world of big power politics; the threat of nuclear
annihilation; the growing gap between the rich and the
poor, among the nations and within each nation; the continuing marginalization of millions of people — all these influenced the choice of the theme.

There was the general conviction at the conference that
we could not speak or think about God's kingdom without
concentrating our thought and our prayer on the situation
of the poor of the earth today. The Bible studies reinforced
that conviction. They led the participants to rediscover
God's special concern for the poor, the down-trodden and
the marginalized. Jesus' own ministry could not be
understood outside of his powerlessness and his identification with the poorer sectors of his society. He went to die
outside the gates to express his belonging to the periphery,
to those who were nothing in the eyes of the powerful. This
spiritual awareness of Melbourne was undergirded by
social, economic and political analyses which made clear
that poverty has nothing to do with God's will. Poverty is
not a matter of fate; it is the consequence of the organization of national and international relations. It has to do
with the relations of state, trade, dominion, dependence,
class, and the exploitation that prevails in the world of nations and within every nation. Christians are called to tackle
this issue from the perspective of the kingdom of God.
Challenged by Jesus' own identification with the poor, we
can no longer consider our own relation to the poor as a
social ethics question; it is a gospel question. Our love for
our neighbour becomes concrete in our transactions with
the poor. For many of us this implies a recognition of our
share in the collective guilt — whether it is on the part of our
country, or of our social class which benefits from the
prevailing situation.

The poor of the earth were seen as the "sinned against".
We are all sinners, the rich and the poor alike; that is one
dimension of the gospel. But Jesus looked at the multitudes
with compassion because he recognized them as "sinned

against", as people who were victims of the sins of others. Often in the Old Testament references to poverty or to the poor are also statements on exploitation and oppression.

This concentration on the poor resulted in a spiritual dynamic; the meeting called on the churches to identify with the poor and to become churches in solidarity with the poor. There was also a recognition that the poor, as objects of God's love, should become subjects of their own history, and that the mission of the church should facilitate the organization of the poor and their participation in God's kingdom and in the mission of the church.

In the past twenty years it has been said again and again that the church should be the "voice of those who are voiceless". This was a necessary function. But there was an element of paternalism in that role. What is more important is to help the poor to organize themselves so that they can make their own voice heard. God's call to conversion is addressed to persons who must respond to it as persons. It is a call to play a protagonist role. To take this seriously in the life of the church is to suggest that the poor should become the real evangelizers. It envisions a movement of the Spirit of God among masses of poor people in the world who are able to evangelize the poor. Through the evangelization of the poor, a calling to repentance, to solidarity, and to new life comes for all persons and for all sectors of society.

Jesus established a clear link between the coming of the kingdom in him and the proclamation of the good news to the poor (Luke 4:18; 7:22). The churches cannot neglect this evangelistic task. The world's poor, who form the majority of people, are waiting for that witness of the gospel which will really be good news for them.

At the Melbourne conference we began to discern something that is of vital importance to all those concerned with the world mission of the church. When we talk about the poor and when our evangelical friends talk about the "unreached", we are often talking of the same people, because the majority of the poor people of the world are not Christians. So our approach to our neighbours is not so much in terms of their religious convictions but in terms of their total human condition. We address them as persons who are victims of the world's division of power and the world's division of labour, and we address them as persons for whom God has a preferential option, and engage with them in actions which will make that a reality in history. If we believe that Jesus brings good news to the poor, we must faithfully follow up its consequences for the mission of the church. Might it not be that the poor have the "clearest vision, the closest fellowship with the crucified Christ who suffers in them, as with them, and... that today they are the *avant-garde* of the mission of the church?"[10]

But for all of us, poor or not poor, the calling to be in solidarity with the poor raises the question of the structures that create poverty. There is a Christian responsibility to mediate love in the form of justice. If we care for the poor only as victims of poverty and if we avoid addressing the root causes of that poverty, we betray our calling. This indeed is the new discovery — that we cannot limit ourselves to the "direct proclamation of the gospel" unless we take with the utmost seriousness the situation of the people to whom the gospel is proclaimed.

Our evangelical friends are also struck by the fact that the unreached are the poor. I quote from the consultation on "The Church in Response to Human Need", to which we have already referred:

> As we reflected on the nearly three billion people who still have to hear of Christ and his gospel, we were struck by the awesome awareness that most of them are poor and that many are getting even poorer. Millions of these people live in situations where they suffer exploitation and oppression and where their dignity as people created in God's image is being assaulted in many ways. We must be deeply moved by their plight. Our Lord Jesus Christ redeems us from eternal lostness and establishes his Lordship over all of our lives. Let us not limit our gospel then to a message about life after death. Our mission is far more comprehensive. God called us to proclaim Christ to the lost and to reach out to people in the name of Christ with compassion and concern for justice and equity.[11]

---

[10] *Your Kingdom Come: Mission Perspectives*, Geneva, WCC, 1980, p.219.
[11] Wheaton Letter to the Churches, p.15.

The language is different, but the concern and the awareness are the same. We face a human reality that challenges the whole of our Christian commitment. It is impossible to say that one can limit oneself to a spiritual or to a material gospel, because in Jesus Christ and in the actual experience of our missionary work the material and the spiritual gospel are one gospel: the gospel of God incarnate in Jesus Christ, calling us to participate with God in that invasion of love.

"Mission and Evangelism — an Ecumenical Affirmation" [12]
The Ecumenical Affirmation on Mission and Evangelism issued by the World Council of Churches is the result of a long process of consultation with member churches, specialized organizations, and theologians of many persuasions. The Affirmation begins with the eschatological vision of a new earth and a new heaven — as the inspiration behind all Christian activity in history. It passes on to a recognition of the enormity of human sin. The two together provide a framework to understand the urgency of the mission of the church — to call people and nations to repentance, to announce forgiveness of sins and a new beginning in relations with God and with neighbours, through Jesus Christ. Evangelization is affirmed as a central dimension of the life of the World Council of Churches, which is itself described as a pilgrimage towards unity under the missionary vision of John 17:21: "so that the world may believe that thou hast sent me".

The freedom of the church in the fulfilment of its mission derives from the freedom we see in Jesus and in the New Testament church. Through participation in God's love, the church is enabled to respond in love to every situation. The church is invited to an identification with humankind in loving service and joyful proclamation, in order that it may fulfill its priestly role of offering intercessory prayer and eucharistic worship.

The starting point of our proclamation is Christ and Christ crucified. Christ is recognized as the one who took

---

[12] The document has been published as the fourth volume in the Mission Series, WCC, 1983.

upon himself all suffering, sin, and death, making available through his resurrection possibilities of new and full life. "Evangelism calls people to look towards that Jesus and commit their life to him, to enter into the kingdom whose King has come in the powerless child of Bethlehem, in the murdered one on the cross." The document ends with a series of affirmations: these relate to conversion, the gospel to all realms of life, the church and its unity in God's mission, mission in Christ's way, good news to the poor, mission to six continents, witness among people of living faiths, and a vision of the future.

The local and the universal in mission

It is often said that the world has become a global village. The inter-relationship between the local and the universal is easy to see in our day. Every small village in Sri Lanka is affected by the fluctuations of the markets in New York or London. What happens to black people in Southern Africa is an issue in internal political discussions in western Europe and in the United States.

World mission cannot be blind to these realities. A church which supports apartheid in South Africa or is indifferent to it cannot claim Christian credentials to carry on missionary work in other countries. What Christians are doing in a particular geographical area at a particular time affects events in other areas and at other times. This is a lesson we have learned dramatically in the World Council of Churches with the Programme to Combat Racism. When this programme supported African liberation movements struggling for racial justice, it gave rise to protest and criticism in churches in the northern hemisphere.

From a Christian or missionary perspective, however, we cannot be faithful to the gospel of Jesus Christ unless we are with the down-trodden and the marginalized. Boycotting the products of transnational corporations, withdrawing our accounts from banks which support apartheid, lobbying in parliaments or with political parties — all these do not appear like mission. But in the modern world, with all its inter-relations, we cannot be effective unless we express our solidarity both at local and global levels.

Of course, when we open the understanding of the mission of the church to practically every human activity — boycott, support of workers on strike, voluntary farm work in the fields, jail reforms, the rights of the Indians, etc. — the question is posed as to where then is our specific Christian vocation. What is it that the church could contribute which no one else is able to contribute to the human community? What is it that distinguishes the particular participation of the church in this collective struggle, in this international solidarity, in this very secular frontier? How can all this be justified as Christian vocation?

The concern for our neighbour, especially for our poor neighbour, needs to be expressed in ways that are historically relevant and historically effective. We do not love our neighbour to save ourselves. We do not love in order to feel better. We want to express our love in such a way that the situation of our neighbour can be changed. But our solidarity and our identification with the poor is *in the name of Christ*; our actions come out of the Christian community, and they are rooted in the discipline of worship and prayer. Thus these "secular" actions are a kind of testimony. They must be relevant, but they should also point to the source of our participation; they should point towards Jesus Christ. This is integral to a theological understanding of our missionary freedom today. We are free to engage in all kinds of human activities provided that those human activities become entry points to the kingdom, and from there we point in the direction of Jesus.

Unity and wholeness in mission

Let me close this chapter with a reference to a discussion we had at the Sixth Assembly of the WCC in Vancouver. The very first question that was raised at the plenary meeting was asked by a Swedish delegate: Why was there no mention of the word "evangelism" in the report of the General Secretary of the World Council of Churches? Dr Philip Potter's response was brief. He said that every single paragraph of his report had implicitly referred to evangelism; more explicitly there was a call to the churches to become confessing churches.

This brief exchange in the plenary hall of the Assembly is basically around the question as to whether evangelism is a dimension of the whole life of the church or a specific, intentional activity. Is evangelism something that is incorporated in all aspects of the church's life, or is it something that we do consciously? If the mission of the church is concerned with the whole human situation, where is the specific evangelistic vocation of the church?

How do we plan for the preaching of the gospel? Do we organize home or foreign missionary activities in such a way that they are considered *opera ad extra*? Or do they belong to the evangelistic vocation, to the evangelistic significance of everything the churches are doing daily? If all that the churches are doing are entry points into the kingdom, all those actions have a missionary dimension and an evangelistic potential. But if the church has become a self-centred, self-caring community, if the concern of the church is not for the kingdom but for itself, at that moment, of course, the whole dimension of evangelism is lost. Most of the foreign missionary enterprises of the last two or three centuries were organized outside the official church structures because the churches did not respond to that particular call. But biblically, the call to mission comes to the whole church. The whole Christian community is called to assume the responsibility of the body of Christ, to manifest the person of Christ in the world.

The actual realization of this vocation could be through all our activities or through an intentional organization of concrete activities. In both cases, the question should be asked: Do these activities serve the kingdom? Are they entry points into the whole dynamic of the kingdom of God?

The theological symbol of the kingdom will help us to overcome all dichotomies, separations and divisions, and to do justice to the particular emphasis represented in each one of the positions we have described. The entire Bible speaks of the purpose of God's words and deeds as being the revelation of his kingdom and the restoration of his liberating rule.

Because the kingdom is all-embracing, and because the Spirit opens our eyes to the presence of the King in concrete situations and circumstances, we are invited to follow, using our God-given freedom. We are empowered to assume our particular missionary vocations. All of them should contribute to the total economy of the kingdom. Silence or proclamation, action or contemplation, resistance or resignation — these and many other seemingly contradictory terms could be used to focus attention on the manifold possibilities open to Christians and churches in the fulfilment of their mission. What we need is a clear vision of what that mission is all about; and then we must discern how our particular entry into the service of the kingdom of God could relate to other entry points and to the participation of others in the same dynamics of the kingdom.

3. The kingdom in the Bible

The kingdom in Jesus' teaching

The symbol of the kingdom of God is central to the Synoptic Gospels. John the Baptist and Jesus announce the kingdom of God and declare that it is "at hand". It is true that the kingdom symbol does not receive the same attention in most of the other books of the New Testament. We shall come back to this surprising difference between the Synoptic Gospels and the other New Testament books.

The fact that the Synoptic Gospels, written about the same time or soon after the epistles, emphasize the teaching of Jesus on the kingdom of God must point to the centrality of this symbol for Jesus himself. The early church concentrated its teaching and proclamation on the expectation of the *parousia* — the second coming. It worshipped the risen Lord, retelling the stories of the cross of Jesus Christ and his resurrection. Stories of his earthly life and extracts from his teaching were at the same time circulating in a parallel or complementary tradition. The Gospels were produced through the organization of independent accounts that were told and retold again and again to preserve the memory of Jesus.

While the early church, whether of Jewish or Hellenistic origin, interpreted both the acts and sayings of Jesus in the light of its own experience, it is evident that the core of the basic affirmations concerning the kingdom came from Jesus himself. Mortimer Arias calls this teaching of the kingdom the "subversive memory of Jesus"[1] that has remained alive and comes, from time to time, to the central attention of the church. We select the kingdom as the central theme around which to organize our understanding of mission because that memory has come back forcefully in our day. It would be difficult to find a more inspiring biblical theme when we face the challenges of the contemporary situation.

Jesus came announcing the kingdom of God to a people living in anticipation of earth-shaking events. Luke and Matthew develop their stories of Christmas in the light of these expectations. Luke describes Simeon (Luke 2:25-32)

---

[1] *Announcing the Reign of God: Evangelization and the Subversive Memory of Jesus*, Philadelphia, Fortress Press, 1984, pp.66f.

as "righteous and devout, looking for the consolation of Israel, waiting for the kingdom to come". When he saw the child Jesus, he was convinced the moment had come: "My eyes have seen thy salvation." Matthew tells of the wise men coming from the Orient looking for a new-born king in Herod's palace. The massacre of children shows how seriously rumours of the coming king were taken by the authorities (Matt. 2:1-18). The time was pregnant with expectation. Inside this world of expectation, and into it, came Jesus. He confirmed and corrected these expectations.

For the three Synoptic Gospels the centre of the preaching and teaching of Jesus was clearly the kingdom of God (of "heaven" in Matthew, but with no difference in meaning). John's Gospel replaces the kingdom with "life eternal", an example of the dynamic translation of a Hebrew concept for Hellenistic readers. Whatever the terms used, the concentration in Jesus' teaching on the symbol of the kingdom is clear; and the kingdom language figured conspicuously in his trial and sentence.

Both Matthew and Luke organize their material carefully; they begin with the expectation and arrival of the king and conclude with the risen Christ assuming the authority of the kingdom and pointing to its future consummation. "All authority in heaven and on earth has been given to me... to the close of the age" (Matt. 28:18-20). In Luke, the disciples ask Jesus: "Lord, would you at this time restore the kingdom to Israel?" The response of Jesus provides a corrective to their understanding of the kingdom which limits it to Israel. It is a promise rather than a description: "You shall receive power when the Holy Spirit has come upon you; and you shall be my witnesses in Jerusalem and in all Judea and Samaria and to the end of the earth" (Acts 1:6-8).

In the Lord's Prayer Jesus taught his disciples to pray for the kingdom (Matt. 6:10), putting this expectation at the core of the religious practice of his disciples. The prayer for the kingdom is completed in a Hebrew parallelism: "Your will be done on earth as it is in heaven." The kingdom for which the disciples are taught to pray is the rule of God over all historical happenings.

In the teaching of Jesus the kingdom of God embraces all the longings and anguished cries of the people of Israel. It responds to the basic message of the Old Testament, and reveals the purpose, character and power of the coming rule of God. It invites people to respond in radical obedience. The proclamation of the kingdom is always accompanied by a call to decision, to follow Jesus, to participate in the mission of God. For Jesus, the coming kingdom is the transforming rule of a compassionate God.

Jesus began with the prevalent expectations among his people. When he preached the kingdom of God, he could build on the idea of the kingdom in the minds of his listeners. He elaborates; he confirms; but he also corrects. Let us first turn to the Old Testament, to discover those basic affirmations concerning the reign of God that were assumed in Jesus' teaching, and then explore how he leads us to a new understanding of the kingdom.

The kingdom in the Old Testament

In the Old Testament the hope of the kingdom has two main historical sources. One is the experience of liberation, and here the Exodus is the focal point. The other is the experience of powerlessness and despair, out of which comes the agonized cry: If God does not save us, who can?

Liberation is followed by celebration and worship, and the establishment of the covenant. God establishes a covenant with the liberated people. It entails a vocation, a calling, and it provides the ground rules for the future relationship between God and God's people.

To liberation and the covenant belongs the prophetic tradition. The prophets denounce the present reality both in terms of the experience of liberation in the past and of the coming day of the Lord. That day would be a day of judgment; but there is always the promise of rebuilding and of re-establishing the people. The prophets reminded Israel of its missionary calling. It is to be faithful to Yahweh, to ensure justice, to care for the weak, to be the people of the promise and of the kingdom. Israel has been established as God's partner in the covenant; through that calling, Israel will be a light to the nations, showing forth God's final purpose of redemption for all.

The other source for the hope of the kingdom is the awareness of God's silence, the experience of the total powerlessness of the people. During the period of the Greek and Roman occupation of Palestine, the odds were heavily loaded against the expectation of the people. They could only wait for God's judgment on history. The apocalyptic literature sees the rule of God as practically absent in present history, but to be fully manifested in the future. There is what amounts to a negation of historical action; living in the present evil situation, the people look forward to the final triumph of God.

In both perspectives, there is a final future that belongs to God. The difference lies in the response to the present situation, in whether one works for approximations to God's rule in the actual conditions of history or acquiesces in the present, depending wholly on the promise of final judgment.

The two lines meet in the Messiah, conceived by the prophets of Babylon as the Suffering Servant. In his missionary freedom Jesus converted the path of suffering and defeat into God's instrument to transform all human history and to attain final victory. He puts himself in the prophetic line, announcing liberation to the people, the year of freedom granted by God. His awareness of the power of the devil and of his own imminent death could be interpreted as the Suffering Servant accepting even the silence of God, which is at the very heart of the apocalyptic perspective. He goes to his death in order to liberate new historical forces to carry out his universal mission.

The kingdom present and future

The reign of God, the kingdom of God in the Old Testament, is to be realized in human history. God is a living God whose will is to be recognized and implemented in the life of the nation.[2] Israel's faith is a historical faith.

---

[2] The term "reign" points to the active, dynamic manifestation of God's royal authority; "kingdom" affirms the same, but introduces the social, communal dimension, the total, transformed reality of the nation and even of nature.

An excellent example of this historical understanding of the kingdom of God comes from the period of the Judges. The faith of Israel in Yahweh as King had its political consequences.[3] The tribes that came from Egypt into Canaan could not conquer the promised land at a single stroke. They first occupied the hills; they were not strong enough to take possession of the valleys. Soon they were joined by people who had escaped from the villages in the valley to find refuge among the Hebrew people in the mountains. The tribes of Israel constituted a loose association of villages kept together by their faith in the lordship of Yahweh expressed through the covenant. They rejected all central authority; their only authority was Yahweh, and the only law was the law that had taken shape in the difficult years of the Exodus. In political language, this was Israel's revolutionary role: to realize Yahweh's kingdom in the land of Canaan. In moments of danger, the villages sought a measure of military unity and looked for a "judge" who would lead them into battle. It was under much pressure that they went to Gideon to ask him to become king over Israel. He would not. He said to them: "Yahweh rules over you" (Judges 8:22-23). Later on, when the elders of the people asked the prophet Samuel to anoint a king for them, he warned them of the sad consequences that would follow (1 Sam. 8:4,5,10,17). A similar example of that historical faith in Yahweh as King is provided by Joshua 24:14,18. Joshua calls the people to make up their mind: if they want to serve Yahweh, they cannot serve other lords. He and his house know what they will do. The unique loyalty to Yahweh involves a clear rejection of all kings from outside or from within. The attitude of the early Christians towards the cult of the emperor and their affirmation that Jesus alone is Lord have their parallels in the Old Testament.

Here is more than the rejection of authority; here is also the recognition that the protection and justice Israel enjoyed should be extended to the strangers and to the weak (Exod. 22:20-23). The jubilee year proclamation (Lev. 25) was the built-in legal provision to ensure that justice prevailed

---

[3] George Pixley, *God's Kingdom*, London, SCM Press, 1981.

— especially in the ownership of land by every family. These laws and the kind of injunctions included in Joshua 24 are important in understanding the ministry of Jesus and Paul's message of justification, new beginning and personal faith. They do not constitute a "spiritualization" of the Old Testament; they attempt to translate these basic perspectives into new historical situations.

There is no complete coincidence between the facts of history and the rule of God, but God actively participates in the shaping of human history, calling, rebuking, correcting, inspiring. The prophets do not provide an interpretation of history as an intellectual exercise but remind people of the obedience that God expects and demands. They announce the coming judgment of God. They demand repentance to be expressed through historical actions of reparation. It is in history that anticipations of the kingdom are experienced and the calling to live in the new day of Yahweh is heard.

The kingdom of God is an invitation to see, beyond the present realities, the power of the age to come, and to find in that power the inspiration to confront the actual historical ambiguities. God calls people to go forward, to look for the new land, for the new justice. The vision of the kingdom, even if based on a historical experience of the past — the oppression in Egypt and liberation from it — is always related to the future. Even historical experiences of failure did not militate against the messianic hope.

The prophetic tradition is sometimes utopian in describing the new reality that God promises but, precisely for that reason, the new reality becomes the people's historical task. The prophets speak of a future that is coming as judgment and promise, but in the light of that future, there is also the call to repentance, new faithfulness and new justice.

History is the scene of conflict with evil, sin, oppression and injustice. It is also where the anticipation of the kingdom is experienced and the summons to live in a new day, the day of Yahweh, are heard. God's final purpose is the establishment of God's peace, shalom. It involves the full implementation of God's justice, the establishment of right relations with one another, with God and with nature. The jubilee year provided for periodic correction of prevail-

ing injustices. The kingdom of God looks to the consummation of history, in and through a dynamic historical process
in which God is the final and deciding protagonist.

The intervention of God is absolutely necessary to bring
to an end the ambiguities of history and the contradiction of
human disobedience, and to incorporate nature in the new
reality. But the vision of the prophet is always historical and
concrete, calling the people to move from Babylon back into Palestine. The shalom of God will be the culmination and
the purification of all human exodus.

The kingdom as rule and realm

The symbol of the kingdom of God has a double
reference all through the Bible. It is the rule of Yahweh and
reminds us of our relation to God as King. Kingship in the
Old Testament indicates the authority of Yahweh, and that
is not limited by geography. It points to the dignity of the
king more than to any particular province over which the
king has dominion. But by extension of that first meaning,
it is also the kingdom of God as a communal concept. The
people as a whole are called to proclaim their loyalty to the
Lord and, consequently, to organize their collective life
within the framework of the law given by Yahweh, the covenant, the decalogue, the jubilee. The first — the affirmation
of God's sovereignty — is basic. To be chosen by God and
to accept God as Lord is to accept God's exclusive claim
on us.

The prophets rebuke the people of Israel because they
have broken their covenant relationship with their God.
Hosea describes it rightly as a violation of human
faithfulness. Perhaps this sense of the absolute sovereignty
of Yahweh was the distinctive feature of Hebrew religion.
God's power was not limited to a particular region or to a
specific aspect of the life of the community. The God of
history was the God of Abraham, Isaac and Jacob, the God
who liberated them from oppression, marched with them
through those difficult years in the desert, and helped them
at every stage in the conquest of Canaan. With this
understanding, the concept of Yahweh as King assumed a
dynamic quality. While the anonymous poet of Psalm 137

could not sing "one of the songs of Zion" in a foreign land, Jeremiah could write to the exiles: "You will seek me and find me, when you seek me with all your heart" (Jer. 29:13). And Deutero Isaiah could proclaim: "In the wilderness prepare the way of the Lord, make straight in the desert a highway for our God... and the glory of the Lord shall be revealed..." (Isa. 40:3-5). To bring out the dynamism of the kingdom symbol, many translators render: "God reigns", "God rules", or "God will save his people".

The calling and promise of God is to Abraham *and* his people (Gen. 12:1-3). Israel is meant to be a light for the *nations*. Peace and justice would kiss each other in the historical shalom of God (Ps. 85). This dialectic of the relation to Yahweh the King and the anticipation of a historical destiny — the working and the waiting for the new city coming from God — is *cantus firmus* of the kingdom in the whole Bible. Personal and communal, historical and eschatological at the same time, it is a vision of the creator God who wants to recreate the people even from dry bones (Ezek. 37:1-14). This dialectic determines the whole Old Testament eschatological hope. The loyalty to God challenges the status quo. The building of the nation is the test of all religious practices in Israel. The justice made visible in interhuman relations will be the evidence of their faithfulness to Yahweh. This double focus of the kingdom in the Old Testament is very helpful in understanding the transition from the proclamation of the kingdom in the Gospels to the proclamation of Jesus in the Epistles.

Israel and the nations

Israel has a universal mission. Israel also has this concrete sense of God's particular relationship with her. Looking back on her history and looking forward to the culmination of God's rule over all creation, Israel was able to discern in Adam and Eve (Gen. 1:26-31), in Noah (Gen. 9:13-17) and later in Abraham (Gen. 12:2-3), the concern of God for all people, all humanity. God is the creator, the sustainer, the judge and the redeemer of all.

The notion of "election" plays a central role in the Old Testament. Yahweh is a personal God, calling a particular people to a specific course of action. Election does not happen because of merit, but because of the mercy of God who hears the "cry of his people" (Exod. 3:7-10). Israel was invited and expected to organize her life in response to that grace. It was — and it is — very easy to confuse election with a sense of ownership. The calling of Israel was to organize a nation where justice would prevail, where the poor, the orphans, the widows, the foreigners would be specially protected (Isa. 1:1-20). The prophets constantly reminded them of their vocation in response to God's election. They referred to God's dealings with other nations and peoples (Amos 1,2) and God's using them for the correction of Israel (Hab. 1). While Israelite nationalism was often reinforced and political manipulations justified by the notion of election, the vision of the prophets was that of a world of nations, all under the loving rule of God.

While the Bible as a whole concentrates on the history of God's relationship with Israel and on the formation of the church, it indicates clearly God's deep concern for the nations. God is the Lord of all nations (Amos 9:7). All nations belong to God (Ps. 82:8). Israel has a vocation to be a blessing to all nations (Isa. 42:6; Jer. 4:2; Isa. 2:3; Mic. 4:2). Chapters 45 and 56 of Second Isaiah make a clear connection between God being the only God and all the nations being called to kneel before him. The promise is that God's "house will be a house of prayer for all people" (Isa. 56:7). God rules over Israel at all times. God blesses, judges, acts through promise and fulfilment, in the concrete events of the people. But the meaning of these extends beyond Israel; they are also to become paradigmatic, sacramental, representative. God's concern for Israel is the concern for a people chosen for a specific purpose; but this very concern —expressed in Israel, through Israel and even outside Israel —embodies God's concern for all other people.

What belongs to Israel is the vocation of being a light to the Gentiles and the nations (Isa. 49:6). God's particularism is rooted in God's universal love. Old Testament history remains for all nations a central point of reference for their own national history. While Israel needs to be reminded that the fact of being children of Abraham does not give them a place in the kingdom, all the other nations are invited to look towards the history of Israel in order to discover clues to understand their own histories.

To summarize, the commanding vision of the Old Testament is the rule of God over the life of Israel and over all creation. Yahweh brought liberation to people in the terrible circumstances of yesterday; Yahweh will bring liberation even in situations today that seem hopeless. He commands history. To believe in God is to respond in obedience, building the community in justice. In fact, Jeremiah goes so far as to affirm that "to do justice is to know God" (Jer. 22:15-16).

This response is made in history. And all of creation will be included in the total transformation that is poetically anticipated. The kingdom demands a personal loyalty to Yahweh and the community Yahweh wills. While the Old Testament concentrates on Israel, it recognizes the place and vocation of all nations under God's sovereign rule. The historical experience and the theological understanding of Israel were thus meant to provide a perspective for all. The memory of liberation and the reality of prevailing oppression together led to the anxious expectation of the coming of the day of the Lord, the arrival of the Messiah. The prophets pointed to the coming of the Messiah, the Anointed One, sent by God to inaugurate the new age. In the apocalyptic literature the image of the Son of Man represented the final action of God, God's intervention in the human drama.

Into that world, charged with hope and fear, Jesus comes announcing: "The time is fulfilled, and the kingdom of God is near at hand. Repent and believe in the gospel" (Mark 1:14-15).

The kingdom in the New Testament

The kingdom is here

Jesus joined John the Baptist and the prophets of old announcing the arrival of the kingdom of God and calling all people to repentance. The new element is the declaration that the time is fulfilled (Mark 1:15) and that *in his own person the kingdom is present and at work*. When Jesus read the scriptures in the synagogue at Nazareth, he amazed the people with the bold claim: "Today this scripture has been fulfilled in your hearing" (Luke 4:21). The messianic promises of Isaiah 61 and 58, woven by Luke into the reading, were manifested in Jesus' actions. His compassion for the powerless represented Yahweh's royal concern for the poor of Israel. The acts of healing and exorcism were powerful manifestations of the kingdom of God. The demons flee, signifying the dawn of the kingdom of God (Matt. 12:28). Jesus forgives sins, and promises a new beginning, as in a jubilee year.

When Jesus sends out his disciples on a missionary journey, he gives them powers related to the kingdom: they are to proclaim the good news to the poor, heal the sick, cast out demons. When they come back and report to him, Jesus interprets what they experienced as a radical defeat of the forces of evil. "I saw Satan fall like lightning from heaven" (Luke 10:18). He tells the Pharisees: "The kingdom of God is not coming with signs to be observed; nor will they say, 'Lo, here it is!' or 'There!' for behold, the kingdom of God is in the midst of you" (Luke 17:20-21).

But such direct references to the breaking in of the kingdom of God in his person and through his acts are not very numerous. The Synoptic Gospels recognize a certain mystery in the person of Jesus and in the manifestation of God's kingdom. They seem to invite people to make up their own minds and come to their own conclusions. When John the Baptist sent his disciples to ask Jesus: "Are you he who is to come, or shall we look for another?" Jesus answered: "Go and tell John what you hear and see: the blind receive their sight and the lame walk, lepers are cleansed and the deaf hear, and the dead are raised up, and the poor have good news preached to them" (Matt. 11:2-5). John should form his own judgment.

Many people did draw their own conclusions; some decided to follow him, "for he taught them as one who had authority, and not as their scribes" (Matt. 7:28-8:1). Others were scandalized, and ascribed his power "to Beelzebul" (Matt. 10:25) or went so far as to conspire to kill him (Matt. 21:46, 26:3). There are hints in the Gospels of the faith of common people; they trust in the authority of Jesus, some leaving everything to follow him. Many of them are foreigners. The exclamation of the Roman centurion by the cross can be taken as a good summary of the response of faith hoped for in the Gospels: "Truly this was the Son of God" (Matt. 27:54). The parables are a teaching aid to help people understand the mysteries of the kingdom. At the same time they are an invitation to discover by faith in the humble beginning of Jesus' life the hidden potential of the kingdom yet to be manifested.

We can feel in the pages of the New Testament the excitement prevailing in the early Christian communities. After the resurrection their faith was confirmed: the authority seen and felt in the Rabbi of Nazareth could not be set aside by the power of the cross. They did not yet have the conceptual categories to explain all these events, but one thing was clear: in this Jesus a radical action of God had taken place, a new age had dawned, and their personal destiny and the destiny of all humankind was now linked for ever to these events.

The kingdom has dawned. The king has visited the people and "will come again". It is amazing that the expectation of the *parousia*, of the coming of Jesus in glory, provides the perspective to interpret the actual life of the Christian community and to read back into the life of Jesus the manifestation of his kingship. For the New Testament as a whole, the life, death and resurrection of Jesus are a powerful evidence of the kingly rule of God in action. A decisive battle has taken place, and it has changed the human situation; a new era has dawned. Christ will come again; but the kingdom has already been made manifest in history, and from that moment on the whole human situation has been already transformed. Meanwhile Jesus has been exalted, and every tongue should confess that "Jesus Christ is Lord, to the glory of God the Father" (Phil. 2:5-11).

A new, radical dimension has been added to the kingdom perspective of the Old Testament. A particular person in a concrete historical period becomes the embodiment of God's final purpose for all creation. Through the coming of the Holy Spirit the Christian community is empowered to remember him, to experience his presence here and now, and to look forward to his coming in judgment and glory. In order to proclaim this faith, they are ready to confront the Jewish authorities and to challenge the imperial pretensions of Caesar. The lordship of Christ is at the very centre of the New Testament vision of the kingdom of God. In him, "once for all" (Heb. 9:26) the foundation stone of the kingdom has been laid.

The battle for the kingdom

The whole life and ministry of Jesus was a continuing confrontation with the powerful of his day. Matthew tells the story of Roman soldiers looking for the child born to be king and murdering all the children under two in that region (Matt. 2:16-18). In Luke's story Simeon describes the conflictual nature of Jesus' vocation: "Behold this child is set for the fall and rising of many in Israel, and for a sign that is spoken against (and a sword will pierce through your own soul also) that thoughts out of many hearts may be revealed" (Luke 2:34-35).

Jesus puts himself in the prophetic tradition, and suffering and persecution belong to his vocation. He also incorporates in himself the apocalyptic tradition that describes end-time calamities; he goes through those calamities by submitting himself to the trial and the cross. Even if we take the anticipations of the death of Jesus Christ in the Gospels as resulting from the post-resurrection reflections of the early church, it is clear enough that Jesus did not try to avoid confrontation. On the contrary, he did not hesitate to expose the hypocrisy of the powerful, to denounce the exploitation of the poor, and to empower them with the promise of the kingdom.

A great debate divides the interpretations of the gospel with regard to the political character of Jesus' ministry. Even if we do not see Jesus as a political revolutionary, as many do, it is abundantly clear that his prophetic and messianic vocation led him to confrontation with the historical forces of oppression and the powers and principalities of his day.

As Leonardo Boff points out, politics as a limited, partial, particular field of human activity cannot describe the total richness of Jesus' life:

> He is indeed the Messiah-Christ, but not one of a political nature. His kingdom cannot be particularized and reduced to a part of reality, such as politics. He came to heal all reality in all its dimensions, cosmic, human, social. The great drama of the life of Christ was to try to take the ideological content out of the word "kingdom of God" and make the people and his disciples comprehend that he signified something much more profound, namely, that he demands a conversion of persons and a radical transformation of the human world; that he demands a love of friends and enemies alike and the overcoming of all elements inimical to God and humankind.[4]

The kingdom of God, God's power, was active in Jesus for the benefit of his fellow citizens. Jesus took seriously the historical predicament of his nation and, at the same time, in his life, God was working out the divine purposes for the whole of humanity. There are not two different histories, one secular and the other religious. Jesus' was a very down-to-earth ministry. This ministry was for the blessing of Israel; it was at the same time for the benefit of the whole of humankind and to reveal to all nations God's saving will.

In Jesus we have the kingdom in action. He takes as his main vocation the jubilee year proclamation and its implementation in the person of the Suffering Servant. His whole life, till his death on the cross, is a complete manifestation of God's kingdom of love. In Jesus, as in the Old Testament, God is the defender of the forgotten and the marginalized of society. By receiving sinners and outcasts, caring for Samaritans and Gentiles, he comes into conflict with the prevailing forces of society. It was only to be expected that his strictures on the observance of the Sabbath and his attitude to the temple, the symbol and centre of the internal oppression of the Jewish people, would anger the religious leaders.

The International Ecumenical Congress of Theology held in February 1980 in Brazil says in its final document:

---

[4] *Jesus Christ Liberator*, Maryknoll, NY, Orbis, 1978, p.60.

The kingdom that Jesus points to with his messianic practice is the efficacious will of the Father who desires life for all his children (Luke 4, 7:18-23). The meaning of Jesus' existence is to give his life so that we all might have life, and abundantly. He did this in solidarity with the poor, becoming poor himself (2 Cor. 8:9; Phil. 2:7) and in that poverty announced the kingdom of liberation and life. The religious elite and political leaders that controlled Jesus' people rejected this gospel: they "took from their midst" the Witness to the Father's love, and "they killed the Author of Life". Thus the "sin of the world" reached its limit (Acts 2:23, 3:14-15; Rom. 1:18-3:2; John 1:5, 10-11; 3:17-19).

But God's love is greater than human sin. The Father carries his work forward, for the Jewish people and for all the peoples of the world, through Jesus' resurrection from the dead. In the risen Christ we have the definitive triumph over death, and the first fruits of "the new heaven and the new earth", the city of God among humankind (Rev. 21:1-4).[5]

The whole world, even the whole of creation, is the battlefield of the kingdom. Politics has no privileged position, but it is not excluded either. The affirmation of the love and justice of the kingdom led Jesus, and will lead Christians, to conflictual situations. How did Jesus meet such situations?

The suffering Lord

The evangelists give what appears disproportionate space for the story of the crucifixion. Paul says, summing up his own mission: "I decided to know nothing among you, except Jesus Christ and him crucified" (1 Cor. 2:2). There, on the cross, the present and the future meet. The cross marks the climax of a historical conflict. But the cross is also the focal point of the divine-human drama. The New Testament affirms that through his death Jesus confronted all forces of evil, oppression and death and, vindicated by God in the resurrection, is now proclaimed victorious over all powers and principalities.

The cross was the consequence of the social and political struggle in which Jesus was engaged. His love for the outcasts, his preference for the poor, his proclamation of

---

[5] *The Challenge of Basic Christian Communities*, Sergio Torres and John Eagleson eds, p.236.

God's kingdom as manifested in him would not go un-challenged. He could perhaps have avoided the cross by making concessions to the authorities, but he would not. The non-resistance that he preached was lived to the end. All this is very historical, very political; but at the same time, through the same events, the drama of God's saving and liberating will for all people was being disclosed.

Whether we use historical and political language or apocalyptic language, we are describing the same reality. The morning of the resurrection confirms that both the hidden negative forces and their historical manifestations in Israel have been defeated. Evil at its worst could not extract from the crucified one a word of hate. Evil has been dethroned by the suffering of the innocent one. Of course, there still are tragic manifestations of evil in human history, but evil has been defeated. The followers of Jesus know that there can be no completely hopeless situation because hope has triumphed on the cross.

This applies also to the kind of evil which we know as oppression, with its consequence of poverty and suffering. The apostle Paul could say that Jesus became poor so that out of his poverty all of us could become rich (2 Cor. 8:9). No situation of poverty is now final. It does not correspond to God's will, and it is condemned. It needs to be challenged. And the final enemy, death, is also defeated. This is the revolutionary affirmation of the Christian faith. In Jesus Christ, the power of the kingdom was at work, transforming the whole of human history. The rule of God has now been vindicated — over death, misery and evil. The new people of God are called to proclaim these events and to give hope to all humankind.

It is in this context that we should understand the differences between the preaching of the kingdom of God in the Gospels and the announcement of Jesus as Lord and Saviour in the Book of Acts and in the Epistles.

The differences are due to a double process. On the one hand there was the tendency to interpret the meaning of the life of Jesus in the light of the resurrection and the coming of the Holy Spirit, and on the other there was the attempt to translate the symbols belonging to the Palestinian culture

62

and religious background into categories belonging to the
Greek culture and Mediterranean religions. For Luke (Acts
8:12; 28:23) the theme of the kingdom is linked to the
recognition of Jesus as the Christ. Paul mentions the word
"kingdom" only twelve times, but his use of the word is in
complete harmony with the affirmations of the Synoptic
Gospels. He sees the kingdom in concrete actions; he
recognizes Jesus as the foundation of the kingdom; he is
aware of the conflict that belongs to the kingdom; he is convinced about the future vindication of the kingdom (Rom.
14:17; 1 Cor. 4:20; Col. 1:13; 1 Cor. 15:25,50, etc.). The
reality of God's reign, as became evident in the exaltation of
Jesus Christ, informs the letters of Paul even when the word
"reign" or "kingdom" is not used. Jesus stands in clear opposition to all demonic forces. Paul sees this cosmic struggle
against principalities and powers reaching its climax in the
cross and resurrection (1 Cor. 2:8; Eph. 1:21; Col. 2:15).
Here we have both the post-resurrection interpretation of
the cross and the use of Hellenistic terms to render it more
intelligible. As one writer puts it:

> It is central to the biblical word that precisely the One whom
> the principalities and powers crucified (1 Cor. 2:8) is now their
> Lord and Master. The risen Jesus is Lord of the world as well as
> the church. Every strand of New Testament literature boldly
> proclaims this message. "All authority in heaven and on earth
> has been given to me," the risen Jesus told his disciples (Matt.
> 28:18). In Colossians 2:10, Paul declares that Christ is the head
> of the principalities and powers. The resurrected Christ is "far
> above all rule and authority and power and dominion, and
> above every name that is named, not only in this age (i.e., cer-
> tainly in this age!) but also in that which is to come" (Eph.
> 1:21). First Peter also reminds us that angels, authorities and
> powers are now subject to Christ (3:22). Likewise the author of
> Hebrews declares that everything is put in subjection under
> Christ (2:8,9). Nowhere is this stated more powerfully than in
> the Book of Revelation where it is repeatedly affirmed that the
> risen Jesus is now "ruler of kings on earth" (1:5). Even now He
> is King of kings and Lord of lords (19:16; 17:14).[6]

---

[6]Ronald Sider, *Christ and Violence*, Scottdale, Herald Press, 1979,
pp.56-57.

But it is also when faith proclaims Jesus as Lord (Phil. 2:5-11; 1 Cor. 12:3) that we need to call to mind the relation between the kingdom and suffering as God's chosen way. How far the song of the servant, especially Isaiah 53, influenced Jesus is still being debated by scholars. But it cannot be denied that through the centuries the church has seen this connection, and that the actual text of the gospel supports it. It is in Isaiah 53 that we find the highest perception in the Old Testament of liberation through vicarious suffering.

To us this connection is very important because the liberation proclaimed in Isaiah 53 is an integral salvation that involves justification, healing, liberation from oppression, prosperity, peace and koinonia — and eternal life!

The obedience of Jesus unto death, his participation in the poverty and in the oppression of humankind reveals the magnitude of his love, the all-embracing scope of his mission and the power of redeeming suffering in history.

The kingdom to come

We have referred earlier to the new theme introduced by Jesus — the time is fulfilled, the kingdom is at hand. We have also considered the dynamic historical character of the struggle of the kingdom. Now we further realize that the early Christians were full of the expectation of the kingdom to come, the second coming, the judgment, and the transformation of all reality. The prevailing spiritual and theological atmosphere of the early Christian communities was one of praying and waiting for the return of Jesus. The Synoptic Gospels provide evidence that this expectation was shared by Jesus himself. At the same time that he was acting in the power of the kingdom — being himself the kingdom — he called the people to prepare themselves for the radical novelty of its final coming. He used the apocalyptic image of the Son of Man, poor and powerless, coming with divine power to judge all people and to inaugurate the kingdom. Most of the parables of the kingdom point to this future coming. The mystery of the kingdom is its inconspicuousness, small like mustard seed (Matt. 13:31ff.) but it is full of explosive potential.

64

The prayer of Jesus maintains the dialectic between the kingdom we pray for and the will of God that is to be implemented on earth. God's kingdom is in the future; it will come; we are called to enter it. But the kingdom is also at work. This dialectic is explained thus by the author of *Jesus of Nazareth*:

> We must not separate the statements about future and present, as is already apparent from the fact that in Jesus' preaching they are related in the closest fashion. The present dawn of the kingdom of God is always spoken of so as to show that the present reveals the future as salvation and judgment, and therefore does not anticipate it. Again, the future is always spoken of as unlocking and lighting up the present, and therefore revealing today as the day of decision. It is therefore more than a superficial difference, more than one of degree, concerned, so to speak, only with the quantity of colour employed by the apocalyptic painter, when one notes that Jesus' eschatological sayings do not describe the future as a state of heavenly bliss nor indulge in broad descriptions of the terrors of the judgment. Hence in Jesus' preaching, speaking of the present means speaking of the future, and vice versa.
>
> The future of God is *salvation* to the man who apprehends the present as God's present, and as the hour of salvation. The future of God is *judgment* for the man who does not accept the "now" of God but clings to his own present, his own past and also to his own dreams of the future. We might say with Schiller: "What we have denied the moment, eternity will never give back." Only here it applies in a new and fulfilled sense. In this acceptance of the present as the present of God... pardon and conversion are one in the works of Jesus.
>
> God's future is God's call to the present, and the present is the time of decision in the light of God's future. This is the direction of Jesus' message. Over and over again, therefore, we hear the exhortation: "Take heed, watch" (Mark 13:33-37; cf. 5,9,23, etc.). This "take heed to yourselves" (Mark 13:9) stands in marked contrast to all curious questioning. Therefore, those very words of Jesus which refer to the future are not meant to be understood as apocalyptic instruction, but rather as eschatological promise.[7]

---

[7] Günther Bornkamm, *Jesus of Nazareth*, New York, Harper & Row, 1960, pp. 92-93.

Many of the sayings of Jesus concerning the future kingdom come to us in apocalyptic language. However, in comparison with the apocalyptic writers of his time, Jesus himself exercised tremendous restraint. He refused to provide dates, he refused to speculate. And the intention of his teaching through the parables is clear.

— The kingdom is a gift of God. The ethical demands made and the blessings offered by Jesus derive from the assurance that God has decided to bring the kingdom. God's coming does not depend on human strategies. The tragedy of the present situation is not the whole of reality; the kingdom is coming — and that is an invitation to trust.

— The invitation does not kill human initiatives; in fact it invites people to prepare themselves for the kingdom: watch, be ready (Matt. 24:44, 25:10-13; Luke 12:35-37). We must be alert, especially because when the king comes in glory, we shall be judged in terms of our previous, unexpected and even unrecognized encounters with God in history in "these little ones" (Matt. 25:31-46).

— The servants of the kingdom should persevere in spite of failures and difficulties. The final harvest is guaranteed (Matt. 13:3-8). "My word shall not return empty" (Isa. 55:11).

— The kingdom is the highest value to which all others are to be surrendered (Matt. 6:33, 13:44-46).

— Opposition is to be expected. There can be no elimination of ambiguity in history. This is the time of God's patience, the time to repent. The day is coming when all truth will be revealed and it will be a great surprise for all (Matt. 7:21-23; 13:24-30).

In Jewish expectations, the coming of the Messiah meant the breaking in of the shalom of God, the arrival of God's kingdom. With the resurrection of Jesus we have a different understanding of the end of time. The resurrection opened up a new age; it marked the beginning of the eschatological missionary era. There is a period between the arrival of the Messiah in suffering and the coming of the Messiah in triumph. The final arrival of God's kingdom will take place after the completion of the missionary period. From now on the kingdom will have a double reference. First, something radically new has already happened in Jesus; the world has been reconciled to God. All people are called to recognize themselves in this event. Second, living in the present historical period, we are called to look forward to the fulfilment of all the hopes of Israel in the culmination of history, the judgment and redemption of history that will take place in God's own time.

This expectation of the kingdom that permeates the life of the early church, rooted in the experience of the lordship of Christ, enlarges the horizon of faith to embrace the whole of human history and its final destiny. Paul and the other writers of the New Testament mediate the hope of a total transformation of creation — a new heaven and a new earth. The prophets' utopia of universal shalom is thus reaffirmed in the wider context of a universal mission.

The mission of the kingdom

There is a certain consensus that Jesus conceived his mission and the mission of his disciples as being confined to Israel (Matt. 10:5). Perhaps he shared the Old Testament expectation that the nations will come to worship in Jerusalem. The cleaning of the temple courts reserved for worship by foreign pilgrims and the parables of the banquet of the kingdom (Matt. 8:11; Luke 14:16-24) support this view.

However, the whole ministry of Jesus was geared to the overcoming of all human barriers. He clearly rejected the prevailing notion that the promise of God's salvation was limited to the Jewish people. John the Baptist had declared that God could raise children of Abraham from stones (Matt. 3:9). The hero of one of Jesus' central parables is a despised Samaritan. The most impressive testimonies of faith are given by foreigners, like the centurion (Matt. 8:10), the Syrophoenician woman (Mark 7:25), the soldier who saw him die (Matt. 27:54). In the great parables of the judgment (Matt. 25:31-46) *"all people* will be assembled before the Son of Man"; at the very beginning of his ministry he provoked the wrath of the people in Nazareth by reminding them of God's blessing to the foreigners (Luke 4:24-27).

We must conclude that for Jesus the kingdom involves the nations of the world, though he understood his own historical mission and the immediate mission of his followers as centred in Israel. Nor can we dispute Jesus' special preference, among his own people, for the poor and the marginalized.

> The people who receive help from Jesus are... people on the fringe of society, men who, because of fate, guilt or prevailing prejudice, are looked upon as marked men, as outcasts: sick people who, according to the current doctrine of retribution, must bear their disease as a punishment for some sin committed; demoniacs, that is to say, those possessed of demons; those attacked by leprosy, "the first-born of death", to whom life in companionship with others is denied; Gentiles, who have no share in the privileges of Israel; women and children who do not count for anything in the community; and really bad people, the guilty, whom the good man assiduously holds at a distance.[8]

In the Acts the church is described as learning the implications, for its life in the world, of Jesus' coming. It took many disturbing events to convince the early church of its cross-cultural vocation. When the Holy Spirit came upon them at Pentecost, the disciples were able to communicate with the pilgrims and worshippers in Jerusalem. Persecution scattered the Christians; it also gave them an opportunity to explain the happenings in Jerusalem to more inclusive groups. A special revelation turned Saul, the hated persecutor, into Paul the apostle to the Gentiles. The visions of Peter and Cornelius meant a real breakthrough in the understanding of the inclusiveness of the kingdom of God. As their understanding of the meaning and expectation of the *parousia* changed and as they grew in their sense of the true significance of the cross and the resurrection, they were able to articulate a vision of the kingdom as embracing the whole oikoumene. It marked the great leap from centripetal to centrifugal mission.

The great commission summarizes the experience of the early church in relation to the risen and exalted Christ. "All

---

[8] Bornkamm, *op. cit.*, p.79.

authority in heaven and on earth has been given to me. Go therefore and make disciples of all nations, baptizing them in the name of the Father and of the Son and of the Holy Spirit, teaching them to observe all I have commanded you, and lo, I am with you always, to the close of the age" (Matt. 28:18-20).

The horizon expands. Its centre is the faith that Jesus Christ is King of kings and Lord of lords (1 Tim. 6:15), that he fills all things (Eph. 1:23, 4:10), and in him "all things will be united" (Eph. 1:10). The mighty acts of God will result in a "new heaven and a new earth". And to the new Jerusalem the "kings of the earth shall bring their glory, the glory and the honour of the nations" (Rev. 21).

The church and the kingdom

The easy and frequent remark that Jesus preached the kingdom and the result was the church could be taken as a useful rhetorical challenge to faithfulness, but in no sense is it historically or theologically true.

Jesus gathered around him disciples, in different numbers and categories, in order to continue the pro- clamation of the coming kingdom — the twelve, the seventy, the many. These disciples later became witnesses of the resurrection and developed an awareness of their mission as followers of Jesus and in the expectation of his second coming.

Jesus called the whole people of Israel to repentance and to a new life-style which will be in keeping with the coming kingdom. The disciples responded to this call and were ready to sacrifice everything in order to follow Jesus. Of course they were afraid, especially during the days im- mediately after the crucifixion of their master. Nor could they understand the full meaning of the resurrection. They experienced both the joy of his presence and the fear of persecution.

In the Book of Acts, we have a description of the early Christian community. They experienced the presence of the Holy Spirit which produced in them an abiding sense of joy. They lived in fear of those who were determined to obliterate even the memory of Jesus.

In joy and fear they constituted a community of mutual support. There were no needy people among them. Little by little they were led to discover the wider dimensions of their being at the service of the kingdom and their life began to be marked by loving care of others (Acts 3:1-7). They gave fearless witness to the lordship of Jesus when confronting the authorities (Acts 4:19-20). They proclaimed the "word of God with boldness" (Acts 4:31). As Christians continued to grow in number and spread beyond Jerusalem, and their expectation of the kingdom deepened, the self-identity of the church became more and more evident. There was a process of institutionalization at work, but there was also a growth in self-awareness and in response to new challenges. Thus Paul developed the image of the body (1 Cor. 12), first in instrumental terms, showing how the different members could work harmoniously together for the fulfilment of the total ministry; later, in the letter to the Ephesians and Colossians, as the body of which Christ is the head, in a dialectical relation of sharing in the glory of God's plan and being the precious instrument to fulfill a servant role for the benefit of the whole creation.

In the perspective of the kingdom the church is called to be and to go. To be an anticipation of the kingdom; to show in its internal life the values of justice and supportive love; to develop a priestly servant vocation in interceding, in Abrahamic tradition, for the whole human community; to celebrate liturgically, in anticipation, the coming of the kingdom; to watch, like the virgins of the parable, for the coming of the Lord; and then to be the missionary people of God, called and sent all over the world to proclaim and serve, announcing and manifesting the coming of the kingdom of God.

Meanwhile, in the process of Christian living, working towards the kingdom and waiting for the kingdom, the power of the kingdom begins to manifest itself through the Holy Spirit in the transformation that takes place in the lives of Christians. They are invited to participate in the transformation of the whole creation through the guidance of the Holy Spirit. Peter writes of Christians as partaking in the divine nature (2 Pet. 1:4), of the new life in Christ. The kingdom becomes a process of conversion and sanctification. It manifests itself in the change of allegiance, in passing from the kingdom of darkness to the kingdom of light, and consequently in the shaping of all things, both in the individual and communal life, towards the plenitude of the kingdom to come.

To sum up, the New Testament continues to live in one history: in Jesus, in the history of occupied Israel; in the early church, in the history of a scattered community of believers in the wider Roman Empire. But in every case, Jesus is proclaimed as Lord; the kingdom is manifested in the power of the Spirit, calling Christians to a kingdom-oriented life-style, to live in expectancy of the total redemption, transformation and glorification of this world in God's coming kingdom. Between Jesus' ascension and his second coming, a new people, the Israel of God, the church, is called into being. In one sense, it replaces the old Israel. It is now up to this community to show God's universal care for all nations, to testify to the breaking through of the kingdom of God in the life and death of Jesus Christ.

This community should not repeat the mistake of Israel and take its calling as a private privilege. The calling is to mission. It is to engage in the announcement of the King, Lord Jesus; to challenge in his name all powers that afflict and oppress; to be a priestly people interceding for others, Christ's servant people, projecting Jesus' spirit of love in the world, a waiting people pointing towards the promises of God. The church is sent to love God and neighbour, to follow the path and example of Jesus and, with the assurance of the actual power of his kingship to proclaim, teach, disciple and baptize all nations. The church is sent as a servant to all people, with a priestly, missionary and evangelistic vocation. The gospel of Jesus Christ belongs to all people. The kingdom is the hidden meaning of their history. The church witnesses to the kingdom of God until the end of the earth and until the end of time.

4. The kingdom theme as a theological concern

In 1968 Wolfhart Pannenberg could complain that the kingdom of God was a theme that did not figure in contemporary theology; today it would be difficult to come across a theological search for missionary clarity that is not conducted from the perspective of a kingdom theology. Practically all contextual theologies of the third world attempt to interpret reality — historical, cultural and political — in terms of visions of the future within a kingdom perspective.

It is possible in our present time to cherish a common hope for our world. Because of that, we cannot be satisfied with any theological approach that would interpret our situation — the situation of our nation or our religious group — without reference to the destiny of other people and other cultures. Because the world has become smaller, the vision of God has become bigger. We are convinced that God's concern is for the whole of reality and not just for the particular group to which we belong. The growing pluralism in the world is posing questions that demand a frame of interpretation for both the secular and the religious aspects of reality.

There is a common hope; there is also widespread despair. The new concern with the kingdom theme is also the result of a certain apocalyptism, and of this growing despair over the future of humankind. Only with the vision of the kingdom as a prayer that centres on the promises of a new day in God could one find strength and power to continue in hope.

To take an example, Christians in El Salvador, in their struggle to overcome institutionalized violence, are involved in all the ambiguities of revolutionary violence. Simple Christians, facing death or imprisonment, are in this situation inspired by the hope not born of an understanding of the power factors in the situation, but arising out of the conviction that the present reality does not correspond to God's will, cannot be permanent, and that a new day must come. The vision of the kingdom of God is not the product of their despair; it comes from the Bible they read. It is the response of grace to their despair.

The Trinitarian basis

The full manifestation of the kingdom is in the person of Jesus Christ. In him, the powers of the kingdom are at work. He acts with the authority of the King, forgiving sins and casting out demons. He breaks into the domain of the forces of evil. His death reveals the kingdom's dynamics of love. He takes upon himself the sin, the oppression, the mortality of humankind, and his resurrection marks the victory over evil, suffering and death.

He assumed human flesh, was made sin, became poor, and through his death and resurrection brought new life and the promise and anticipation of the coming kingdom. Because we see the powers of the kingdom in operation in the life of Jesus Christ, we realize that he points, beyond its limited manifestation on earth, towards the deeper mystery of God. Jesus is the revealer of God. Jesus is not self-contained; he faces life and meets death in obedience to the Father and filled with the Spirit. The doctrine of the Trinity is the conceptual formulation of a reality lived by Jesus, experienced by Christians, and affirmed by the church. The doctrine appears in the history of Christian thought to express the experience of the apostles and the early Christians who have seen in and through Christ the reality of a creator God and a sustainer Spirit. Jürgen Moltmann writes:

> The history of Christ is interpreted in the light of its origin. The Gospels relate the story of Jesus as the story of the Messiah sent from God into the world for the purpose of salvation and anointed with the Spirit of the new creation. They present the history of Jesus in the light of his sending, his mission.... The relation between the Jesus of history and the God whom he called Father corresponds to the relation of the Son to the Father in all eternity. The *missio ad extra* reveals the *missio ad intra*. The *missio ad intra* is the foundation for the *missio ad extra*.[1]

The suffering and death of Jesus resulted both from the historical controversy in which he was involved and of the saving will of God. Those who were actors in that history were acting in terms of their understanding of the situation,

---

[1] Moltmann, Jürgen, *The Church in the Power of the Spirit*, New York, Harper & Row, 1977, pp.53-54.

responding to factors of power in society. The events that took place in Jerusalem did really take place. They were historical events. At the same time they revealed the suffering, saving will of the Father. Through the suffering of Christ in history we also see that the God who sent him participates in his suffering. The cry on the cross, "My God, my God, why hast thou forsaken me?" (Matt. 27:46), reveals the suffering of the Son in the silence of the Father; it also reveals the suffering of the Father in the fulfilment of God's deepest manifestation of missionary love in order to recover the fallen creation. God is a passionate lover, and whoever loves, suffers. The only way out of suffering is through reconciliation and rehabilitation. The Holy Spirit works in mysterious ways to call us to reconciliation, pointing to the goal of the kingdom which is life in all its fullness. In Jesus we discern God as a missionary God, reaching out to rescue and save, creating in freedom a relationship of love. The historical kingdom of God takes shape as the Spirit of God calls humankind to a new relationship. Christ represents the expression of God's missionary love reaching out to recover the loyalty, the love and the covenant relationship that was granted in freedom and lost in sin.

The faith in the triune God corresponds to our experience of Jesus Christ and of the coming of the Spirit. Christian reflection on this historical reality led the church to the conviction that it is the manifestation *ad extra* of an internal reality in God. Jesus points towards the creative purposes of God, and towards the redemptive action of the Holy Spirit calling the whole creation to reconciliation. When we talk of the mission of Jesus Christ we are talking of the eternal mission of God. We understand our own mission in the light of the mission of Jesus Christ who was sent by the Father in the power of the Spirit.

The cross tells us that in history the kingdom suffers violence. Because of the cross we cannot live in facile optimism about history. The forces of evil are real. To defeat them God's Son had to be sent. The cross signifies God's recognition of the power of evil. It also shows how God deals with evil. Jesus' encounter with evil leads to the cross, and to the vindication of love in the resurrection. Our

74

mission is the same. The mission of the church is indeed the
continuation of the incarnation. God the Father sends the
Son in the power of the Spirit; Jesus calls the church to
enter into this missionary movement of God.

The sin which resulted in the cross is however present in
all human beings, and does not spare the churches. We can
only put our faith in God's calling, in the indwelling of the
Spirit, on Jesus' promises to be present wherever two or
three meet in his name — and not in a particular quality or
merit of the Christian churches! But the frailty of our condition or the sad reality of our sin should not blind us to our
vocation to become ambassadors for Christ calling
everybody to reconciliation with God (2 Cor. 5:16-21). We
are called to share in God's redemptive passion.

Extraordinary and ordinary mission?

Because the kingdom is the mission of the triune God,
creator, redeemer, sanctifier, it is concerned with the whole
of reality. Nothing, especially nothing human, is outside
this loving concern. God's rule is seen in the preservation of
nature, in the movement of the stars, in the changing
seasons, and in God's care for people. God's care for people
must happen through people. God calls us to love and to
justice, but God is not an agent outside history intervening
always in miraculous ways. The miracle of God's love happens through free human beings who are called to be co-
workers in the working out of God's purposes.

In the words of a Danish theologian, Johannes Aagaard,
God works through one extraordinary mission and many
ordinary missions.[2] The extraordinary mission is the mission of Jesus Christ, the mission of the church —
manifested in the sending of Jesus Christ and in the calling
of the church to its particular vocation of witnessing to the
kingdom of God. The ordinary missions are the missions of
the nations, the missions of all historical agents that
cooperate in the building up of the human community.
Through all aspects of human history — political,

[2]*Mission After Uppsala*, University of Aarhus, Denmark, August 1970,
unpublished paper, p.6.

economic, cultural and social — human beings are called, as communities and individuals, to participate in God's providential care — which includes the building of caring, protective communities.

This distinction is useful, but it cannot be absolutized because Christians and churches are also necessarily involved in the so-called ordinary missions through diaconal ministries. The fact that the church is a social institution has in itself socio-political consequences. The church is called into existence to serve the extraordinary mission, God's own revelation in Christ, but through its very existence it becomes involved in all aspects of God's caring mission for humankind. The distinction is useful insofar as it points to the special responsibility of the church for the extraordinary mission. The recognition of histories other than the history of Israel and of agents other than the church of Jesus Christ as agents of the kingdom of God is itself possible only because of the ministry of Jesus Christ. It is the vocation of the church to proclaim the King and to declare the values, the perspectives, the goals and the signs of the kingdom in such a way that both missions of the kingdom could one day be one — as they already are in God.

The church is the bearer of the secret of God's purpose revealed in Christ. Therefore it has a missionary responsibility to share that knowledge with other agents, who are also serving the kingdom, though they are unaware of it and cannot through their service meet the ultimate demands and goals of the kingdom. It is not that the mission of the church sacralizes secular reality by claiming it for the kingdom. The mission of the church introduces, from the revelation perspective, an element of renewal, of repentance that could enable these agents to become part of the total mission of God — extraordinary and ordinary. We must also recognize that the so-called ordinary mission, the mission of preserving life, is bound up with the extraordinary mission; it is fundamental for the mission of the church. Secular factors and political forces help or hinder the ministry of the church. Roads were constructed in the Roman empire for military or for economic purposes; but it facilitated the spread of the gospel in the first century. A law that provides for religious freedom is not unrelated to the extraordinary mission of God; it creates the frame within which the extraordinary mission can take place. The preservation of life is never just "secular or ordinary", it is visibly extraordinary when those lives enter into living relationship with the God of Jesus Christ through the church. The Persian King Cyrus was an instrument of God, as Second Isaiah saw so clearly.

We could, and should, distinguish between the mission of God through the church, the people who have responded to the call of God in Jesus Christ, and the mission of God through other agents who are promoting aspects of that mission. But from the kingdom's perspective there is a continuum of love between the preservation of life and the new birth of a life of faith.

Conversion to the King, personal and collective

Because the kingdom is God's mission, fully manifested in the total self-emptying of Jesus Christ, those who listen to the message of the kingdom are invited to respond in radical discipleship. Conversion is not an option for the pastoral work of the church. It is the only possible answer to the dramatic disclosure of God's passionate love. To proclaim the kingdom is always an invitation to join the forces of the kingdom and to enter into the kingdom. Repentance is the first act of response. Sins are confessed, allegiances changed and attitudes transformed. If the kingdom is God's plan in action, and if what the Christians experience is the anticipation of that kingdom that is coming into the actual life of today, then we move in a world of wonder and excitement, a world of final decisions. No other word than conversion would serve here. Of course, the word conversion has been misused; it has been reduced to mean a psychological experience. We need to recover the meaning of that word for the act of response to the call of the Servant King, Jesus Christ, that will send us, as the Father sent Jesus, sustained by the Spirit, along the same path of suffering and hope.

In our response to the kingdom we are integrated into the process of life in God. The movement of love from the

Father, Son and the Holy Spirit continues through the church, calling us to be servants and to show the first-fruits of the Spirit. Jesus put the poor and the children at the centre of the concern of the disciples to symbolize the radical demand of love made by God. The prophets, John the Baptist and Jesus held up the poor as the final challenge to test our response to the kingdom. Response to the kingdom could mean abandoning wealth, family and social relations, but never as an end in itself. Renunciations are necessary in order to integrate ourselves into the movement of love which works for the poor and the outcasts. Justice is the response demanded from those who listen to the call of the kingdom; it is a penultimate goal, paving the way for the actualization of the kingdom of love in *history*. Justice in its biblical sense is rehabilitating justice. It is not to give to each one what he or she deserves; it is to provide everyone what he or she needs to enter into the dynamics of the kingdom.

Very often in the Bible, people are spoken of or addressed as a collective entity. Israel is conceived as a whole. Even in the theological treatise on Israel that Paul presents in the letter to the Romans (9-11), Israel is seen as a collective body that has had its existence through generations, and receiving salvation at the end of time, when God will have mercy on all people.

There is a vocation in the kingdom of God for these collective entities — like Israel, Assyrians and Egyptians. They are called to repentance, conversion, obedience. Perhaps Jesus' "death for many" could also be understood along these lines; it is also for the collective realities of cultures and nations.

We speak of the church as one such entity. The church is not a club of individuals who pool their private religious experiences in a common body. The church is the body of Christ. It is a corporate reality preserved through the centuries, into which we are integrated. This element of collective identity is not easy to appreciate in our day because we put so much stress on individualism. To contemporary consciousness it appears not unlike a narrow nationalism. But the family and the nation and all the collective fruits of culture should be considered as the offerings that the kings of the nations bring to the the kingdom (Rev. 21:24). The kings of the earth here are not individual kings who come personally; they stand for their nations, with all their heritage of cultures and values. That corporate reality is also the object of the concern of God. All our sacrifices offered in love for friends, family, humanity are not lost. To spend ourselves in the struggles for justice and peace is not a waste of time and energy. These are all the collective offerings that will be presented to the King of kings. It is important to labour this point because we often tend to forget this collective dimension in our emphasis on personal salvation.

There is of course a personal call. The parables of the kingdom make that very clear. To follow Jesus is to become a new creature in him; it is to taste something of what the Gospel of John calls eternal life, life in all its abundance. It is indeed important that we preserve this individual, personal dimension. Even to work for the corporate good of humankind we need faith commitment and personal conviction.

The prize of the kingdom

We need to recover in our Christian preaching and teaching the belief in resurrection and life after death. Our civilization tends to tone down the reality of death. It is true that an undue preoccupation with life after death could be, in fact has been, a way to evade historical responsibilities. But we cannot deny the testimony of the scriptures concerning the resurrection of Jesus Christ and the promise of eternal life in him and the kingdom through God's final triumph over death. We need to affirm this conviction that life overcomes death in our daily life, and especially in moments of conflict. Julia Esquivel has said:

> Thus the reign of God is the ability to believe until death, and even beyond death, that God is our father and that we are brothers and sisters. It means living so as to break down all divisions, all injustices, to dry every tear, to love in such a way that we may share our lives, because we believe that death no longer has any power over us.
>
> He who believes that on the throne of God the Lamb reigns who was slain for love does not dare kneel down before any god

made of gold or stone. He dares to oppose any political project that produces injustice or death for the people. Although he may die, he has already been resurrected. The kingdom cannot be taken away from him...

For that kingdom Moses renounced the throne of Egypt and preferred to share the ills of the people of God. Others die after being beaten, without accepting the transactions that would have rescued them, because they preferred resurrection. Others suffered the trials of mockery, beatings, and even the chains of prisons. They were stoned, others were tortured, burned, persecuted and discredited. Others are marked so that their movement can be controlled. Others are left without food and land. Others are shot while they bury their martyrs. Others flee to the mountains and find refuge in caves. But all of them, even though they continue to be oppressed and mistreated in the factories, the fields and the cities, march onward, lifting their eyes to the future, towards Jesus from whom they derive their faith and who shall give them their prize. For his sake and for their sake we must resist until death, knowing that he has conquered the world.[3]

That text comes from an experience of confronting death. The sense of fear and trembling, of trust and joy, comes to us because our life has already been taken up by God. The maximum that a human ideology can promise is that the sacrifice of people through the centuries will find its fulfilment in the classless society. It does inspire people to acts of heroic self-sacrifice. But in the Christian eschatological perspective, everyone is invited to give up life in the service of neighbours and in working for love and justice, simply because God cares for history and our service is part of that caring. We do not sacralize history; we surrender our life to God in the knowledge that our personal and collective life will find its fulfilment in the kingdom.

The invitation to the kingdom is addressed to each one because God is a caring personal God. We respond to it because we know that our being now and for ever is in God. We engage ourselves in historical action in the trust, amidst the ambiguity of our involvement, that death cannot defeat God's creative and liberating purpose and that in the power

---

[3] "The Crucified Lord: Latin American Perspective", in *Your Kingdom Come: Mission Perspectives*, Geneva, WCC, 1980, pp.59-60.

of the Spirit even our death could serve God's purposes. This, perhaps, is the wisdom of the pietistic movement that demands a personal experience of God in order to be able to enter fully, joyfully, into the risk of missionary obedience. But when we become content to bask in personal piety and do not involve ourselves in the struggle of the kingdom with all its risks, then faith becomes a sedative and missionary engagement loses its edge.

Offering the "now" of history

The kingdom is coming. We are asked to pray for it. The assurance of that future already conditions our present. The kingdom is the power of the future operating in the present reality.

The kingdom is indeed a present reality. Jesus sends the disciples, and tells them: "All authority, all power, the reign in heaven and on earth has been given to me" (Matt. 28:18-20). As a consequence the disciples go into all regions of the world knowing *a priori* that those regions are already being shaped by the kingdom that has been given to Christ and that is surely coming. Hope becomes a motivation, and the life of the Christian community becomes an anticipation of the power of the kingdom. The Holy Spirit is active, producing the fruits of love that belong to the final manifestation of the kingdom.

The teaching of Orthodox theologians on the transformation of the whole reality on the model of the transfiguration can help us in our understanding of the relation between history and eschatology.

The liturgical celebration is the moment of awareness, of experiencing the beauty of the coming kingdom. It is the anticipation of the kingdom; it is the moment when we offer to God the whole cosmos, society, nature and life, which needs to be transformed. In Jesus' ascension, human nature has been taken up to God. Paul is able to say (Col. 3:3) that "our life is hidden with Christ in God".

This transformation is not an automatic process; it is a continuous search. It is an exposure of ourselves in worship to the action of God. Because we find ourselves, after Jesus' resurrection, in the new aeon, we do not seek merit; our works now are expressions, tainted with sin surely, but nevertheless an offering brought to the altar to be burned, purified and accepted.

What we do today for the sake of the kingdom, what past generations have done, what coming generations will do are all preserved in God's own being. God's faithfulness was the guarantee of the covenant in the Old Testament; it is also the guarantee of the new covenant. The kingdom is the goal towards which God wants to take all history. In this God of the future our *present* is received, purified, and preserved.

There are many failures. We know of a few here and there who paid with their lives in an attempt to change situations of human oppression. But there are many others who have spent themselves in acts of love and whose names do not appear in books of history and the memory of people. In God, however, there is memory. Everything that is of value to the kingdom belongs and remains because the kingdom is God's plan and promise, from the beginning of time; its reality is in the missionary being of God.

Karl Barth affirmed that there is no point of contact built into us that would give us access to God. The reality of sinfulness as described in the Bible, especially in the letter to the Romans, is such that there is nothing in us that could enable us to have access to God. It is only in the God-man Jesus Christ that God established the point of contact with humanity. It is in Christ that we are related to God, *in Christ* and not in ourselves. Therefore I cannot trust in my own experience of conversion and in my own experience of forgiveness. I can only trust in God's grace manifested fully in Jesus Christ and in his promises. By living in Christ in this relationship I am able to say that I have the assurance of my salvation in Christ. But the only *guarantee* is God's love for me and not my love of God. That is the fundamental message of Paul in the letter to the Romans.

"For I am sure that neither death, nor life, nor angels, nor principalities, nor things present or things to come, nor power, nor height, nor depth, nor anything else in creation will be able to separate us from the love of God in Christ Jesus our Lord" (8:38-39). Often we quote this in a spirit of boastfulness, to suggest that there is no power in the world that could destroy our love for Christ. But Paul is not saying that we cannot fail, but that there is no power that can make God fail us! Our life in Christ is guaranteed in God's faithfulness towards us (Col. 3:3).

That faithfulness must extend to our communities as well. What is true for our individual lives should also be true for our collective life. We cannot of course claim that the families we build, the communities we organize and the culture we develop belong to the economy of the kingdom. We enter into these activities in the hope that they will be taken as our offering to the kingdom of God, but finally our trust is in God whose wisdom rejects, accepts and perfects. Precisely because there is this continuity of faithfulness in God, we can engage in many different kinds of activities, knowing that God will apply the criteria of selective love to all we do. As the apostle Paul writes (1 Cor. 15:58): "Therefore, my beloved brethren, be steadfast, immovable, always abounding in the work of the Lord, knowing that in the Lord your labour is not in vain."

The judgment of God will cleanse and transform the offerings we make so that they become worthy of the kingdom. We do not build the kingdom, but we build the human community in the light of the kingdom that is coming. We offer whatever we can produce under the inspiration of the Holy Spirit to be burned on God's altar. Because it is an offering to God, we want to offer the best that we have. Expressions like "building" the kingdom are best understood in terms of our intention to offer to God the best, knowing that God is the one who brings the final shalom, the consummation of all things.

The utter realism of the biblical literature is evident in its proclamation of the kingdom of God as the coming reality. No matter how well things were going, no matter how intimately the communion with God was felt, the kingdom of God was announced as the future, the coming kingdom. In the light of the futurity of God's kingdom, it is obvious that no present form of life and society is ultimate.

This insight does not paralyze political activity. The future kingdom of God — because it is God (for God's being cannot be

separated from his rule) — demands obedience already in the
present. The future of the kingdom releases a dynamic in the
present that again and again kindles the vision of man and gives
meaning to his fervent quest for the political forms of justice
and love. The new forms that are achieved will, in contrast with
the ultimacy of God's kingdom, turn out to be provisional and
preliminary. They will in turn be called upon to give way to suc-
ceeding new forms. Superficial minds might think that the
political quest is therefore futile. They fail to recognize that the
satisfaction is not in the perfection of that with which we begin
but in the glory of that towards which we tend.[4]

Of course this adapting of the present to the promised
future will call for informed action, based on sociological
research and scientific analysis. The approximations we
achieve will be marked by the sinfulness of our situation and
the mistakes arising out of human limitations. We can only
offer the fruit of our labours as an offering that needs to be
purified, and integrated into God's plan, in the wisdom of
God's own will.

We can also say that the penultimate is a preparation of
the way of the Lord. That is the prophetic expression John
the Baptist applied to himself; he came to prepare the way
of the Lord. To apply it to ourselves will appear preten-
tious. But seen from the perspective of the kingdom that is
coming, it is the path of obedience and discipleship.

No human situation is ultimate; every human situation is
penultimate. On this all Christians agree. What we are saying here is that the penultimate human situations assume
ultimate significance because God is interested in this
penultimate. God is active in word and sacraments and is
present in the poor waiting for our response to God. Our
responses are indeed relative, ambiguous and penultimate,
but they become ultimate because of the hidden and yet
revealed presence of Christ. And within that reality the
judgment on each situation is a final, ultimate judgment!
We cannot pretend that anything that we do corresponds to
the final reality of the kingdom of God. But we engage
ourselves in action with all seriousness because the God of

---

[4] Wolfhart Pannenberg, *Theology and the Kingdom of God*, Philadelphia,
Westminster, 1969, pp.80-81.

the kingdom seeks our response and our obedience. This is what takes all religions in general, and Christianity in particular, to the verge of fanaticism and intolerance; a relative situation becomes an ultimate situation in the perspective of God's presence! We need to recognize the relativeness of each situation; we need to be reminded of its penultimate character. The kingdom that is coming is the final critique of all our historical reality. But we offer in trust the fruit of our labours.

"Your kingdom come"

The New Testament links the kingdom to the realm of prayer. There are two prayers that need to be kept in constructive tension: "Your kingdom come" and "Maranatha, come Lord Jesus" — the prayer of Jesus and his disciples and the prayer of the early church. Our understanding of the kingdom as God's plan from the beginning of time and part and parcel of God's own missionary being, expressed in creation, liberation and redemption, culminating in the ministry of Jesus, fills us with wonder, and we can respond only in worship. We are transported into a reality that permeates all creation. Prayer is the only language to express such mystery; even our theological reflection on the kingdom needs to be done in prayerful conversation with God. In this sense, the kingdom is a spiritual reality. But the word "spiritual" does not mean "separated from reality". It points to the presence of God and the freedom of the kingdom, and gives meaning to the whole of reality. The kingdom that we pray for is the kingdom that incorporates the promises of the final shalom of God in historical situations.

The second prayer, Maranatha, is a necessary reminder that we are waiting for the kingdom of *God* and that we cannot be satisfied with the tentative efforts that we offer for the implementation of the kingdom in history. Our prayer is for the coming of the *King* whose presence, fully manifested, is the mark of the kingdom. Bishop Lesslie Newbigin remarked that it is easier for Christians to pray "Your kingdom come" than to pray "Maranatha".[5] In the

---

[5] *Your Kingdom Come, op.cit.,* pp.41-42.

kingdom concept, we rightly include most of the basic aspirations of humankind for peace and justice which exist even independently of the Christian revelation. But we are praying for the kingdom of God, for the kingdom manifested historically in Christ and coming in all its fullness in the return of Jesus Christ. Ideologies can be offerings to the kingdom, but never substitutes for it.

Finally, what is new in the Christian vision of the kingdom is the King, Jesus of Nazareth. He is the Servant King. The centre of our Christian hope is Jesus Christ. This becomes evident as we turn to the mission of the church in the serving of the kingdom and the freedom that belongs to that mission. The King who is coming will be the commanding reference for all our options and priorities, and for the whole of our Christian vocation.

5. Freedom in the mission of the kingdom

We have seen, biblically and theologically, that the kingdom of God embraces the whole of reality, and that nothing historical is foreign to God's creative and redeeming love. Nothing is outside the authority given to Christ as Lord, and no events are outside of the work of the Holy Spirit. We have also seen in Jesus Christ the full historical manifestation of the kingdom, the kingdom in action. By calling him Lord, the early church recognized in him the authority that in the Old Testament belonged to Yahweh, the King.

The invasion of love in history

Jesus is, according to Revelation 1:5, the true witness to God. In his life, his teachings, his death and resurrection, he reveals God's purpose, God's plan which we call the kingdom. He manifests the powers of the kingdom and engages in the final struggle with the powers of the anti-kingdom on the cross. He is the one who witnesses, finally and fundamentally, to God's liberating purposes. He calls the church to assume the vocation of witness. The church's witness is derived from Jesus' own commission: "As the Father has sent me, so I send you" (John 20:21). As he was the witness in the power of the Spirit, so the disciples will receive the Spirit to become witnesses (Acts 1:8). The disciples, and the church they helped build up, are witnesses to God's powerful invasion of love into history in the person of Jesus Christ.

If we want to sum up in a few words the meaning of Jesus, it will be difficult to find a better expression than this — an invasion of love, an outpouring of love, from the incarnation, through his whole ministry, to the cross. His own definition of his mission is found in the passage in Luke 4:18-21; in him is manifested the rehabilitating justice which is one of the biblical definitions of love. He looked on the multitudes with compassion (Matt. 9:36). The Gospel of John summarizes Jesus' mission; of his decision to go to Jerusalem and to the cross the passage says that "having loved his own who were in the world he loved them to the end" (John 13:1).

Jesus said that he came to serve, to give his life as a ransom for many (Mark 10:45). The vocation to be the witness of the kingdom meant a total living out of self-surrendering love. And that love was wholly free in the way it was offered.

A dramatic example of his love and his freedom is seen in this passage: "A great crowd followed him and thronged about him. And there was a woman who had a flow of blood for twelve years, and she came up behind him in the crowd and touched his garment. And immediately the hemorrhage ceased, and Jesus, perceiving in himself that power had gone forth from him, immediately turned about in the crowd, and said, 'Who touched my garment?'"... Then he tells the woman: "Daughter, your faith has made you well; go in peace, and be healed of your disease" (Mark 5:24-34).

Here is the bearer of God's revelation for all time. Here is the prophet who for the multitude was the hope of the coming kingdom. And he stops to respond in love to a woman in distress. The story reveals in a dramatic way the normal attitude of freedom that Jesus had at all times. When he was on the cross, involved in the internal drama of God's own being, he was able to care for the robber at his side and the woman at the foot of the cross. That is missionary freedom — the capacity to respond in love to the need of all.

Freedom in the ministry of love

According to Matthew (4:23ff.), "he went about all Galilee, teaching in the synagogues, and preaching the gospel of the kingdom and healing every disease and every infirmity among the people". It is very difficult to make a distinction between the teaching and the preaching of Jesus; the teaching nature of the healing or the proclamation around the casting out of demons. There is no priority; there is no distinction. This description of Matthew is not normative, but it helps us understand Jesus' vocation.

Jesus teaches, preaches, heals. Perhaps we need to start with preaching because that is what he did, coming after John the Baptist, proclaiming that the "kingdom of God is at hand". His proclamation centres around the kingdom, announcing good news to the poor (Luke 6:20) and denouncing the rich (Luke 6:24), the scribes and the Pharisees (Matt. 23:23-36). He rebukes the political powers (Luke 13:31-35; Mark 10:42). The proclamation of Jesus has a double function; it announces the breaking in of the kingdom of God that brings the good news of redemption and liberation for the poor and the outcast; it also contains a warning of judgment on all those who are powerful in society and reject the call to repentance.

Jesus heals. It is interesting that in this passage from Matthew there is no mention of the fact that Jesus forgives. We give today more importance to the forgiveness of sins than to the healing of the bodies and minds of people. But in the gospel these distinctions do not have much significance. The word "salvation", as used in the Gospels, implies both.

In this relationship between healing and forgiveness we see again the freedom of Jesus. The friends of the paralytic, who go through a great deal of trouble on behalf of the patient, are looking for healing. The man's real problem, from the perspective of his friends, was his ill-health. Jesus, looking at the man, speaks a word of forgiveness. That is a scandal to the Pharisees (Mark 2:1-12) and a disappointment to the friends. Some of the scribes questioned in their hearts: "Why does this man speak thus, it is blasphemy. Who can forgive sins but God alone?" The healing that follows is for Jesus a sign to authenticate the forgiveness. Here is an illustration of the dynamic, creative relationship between forgiveness and healing. We see in the Gospels many who come to Jesus in search of healing, and they receive only healing! Jesus is free in his love to respond to what he sees as the need of the person, and of the situation that the person is facing.

Whether he heals or forgives, Jesus expresses his love in reponse to the concrete situations of people. This is the freedom of love. Jesus feels free, after proclaiming the gospel to the poor, to enter the house of rich people. But the fruits of that encounter with rich people are related to his concern for the poor, as is clear in the story of Zacchaeus (Luke 19).

Jesus teaches, and his teaching is about the kingdom. It is about the quality of life that belongs to the citizens of the kingdom. But his teaching is also contained in actions that must oblige people to rethink their interpretations of the law and the prophets. For example, he breaks the law by healing people on the Sabbath. He feels free to break the law in order to save, to heal, to help. He sympathizes with his disciples when they break the religious law which prescribes they should rest on the Sabbath, and the religious ethical law concerning property. In the freedom of love, he sees the law of need or the law of life as being more important.

Jesus casts out demons; that is to say, he fights the spiritual forces which oppress people and corrupt individual attitudes and the structures of society, so that he may liberate people and society from their power. The all-embracing kingdom of love is the basic guideline. The concrete occasion, the invitation to a kingdom action or a kingdom proclamation, is provided in Jesus' ministry by the needs of the outcast, the powerless and the marginalized.

It is his vocation, the assumption of the burden of the world, which provides unity to his freedom. Each action of Jesus responds to a situation, an opportunity, a need, a challenge. He sees a need and he responds to it. But always it is love in action; it is freedom in action. While each action represents a response to a situation, each one achieves a fuller meaning because of Jesus' own messianic vocation. In the feeding of the multitude, a particular need of the people is met. At the same time, it achieves a richer meaning when it is interpreted as an anticipation of the holy communion, and even of the messianic banquet in the coming kingdom.

Each one of these independent actions points to the whole, which is the revelation of God's love and the inauguration of God's kingdom. For the lame people who were brought to Jesus a discourse on the kingdom could not be an entry point to the kingdom. There were occasions to make long discourses on the kingdom, and Jesus made use of them. He preached regularly in the synagogue; that was part of his normal, ongoing work. Every one of these actions was necessary to point to an understanding of shalom, and all the actions together provided a vision of the promise of God. They enabled people to understand salvation as forgiveness, as healing, as the invitation to follow Jesus, as love of one's neighbour, as the struggle against all powers and principalities, as the affirmation of the freedom of love as against the bondage of law.

Some of the actions of Jesus acquired their full meaning only after the resurrection, because it is only in the light of the whole that the parts can be understood. As a church today, we have the advantage that we know the total story of Jesus; that enables us to apply all parts of the story to the different and particular actions of love which the church is called to develop in specific situations.

The church's witness to the kingdom

The church is called to give witness to the breaking in of the kingdom of God in Jesus. By the indwelling power of the Holy Spirit, it is to be the mirror of the mystery of the kingdom of God. Christians are servants of the whole kingdom; but within the world-embracing dynamics of the kingdom, the special vocation of the church is to announce the kingdom and to invite people to the kingdom. In the Great Commission Jesus first refers to the authority that he has been given, and says to his disciples: "...go therefore and make disciples of all nations, baptizing them in the name of the Father and of the Son and of the Holy Spirit, teaching them to observe all that I have commanded you; I am with you always, to the close of the age." Several other biblical passages deal with this particular responsibility of the church within the total economy of the kingdom of God.

Both the nature of the kingdom that we proclaim and the personality of the King who commissions us make it impossible for us to be satisfied with a purely intellectual proclamation. Because the kingdom is life, Jesus is the living Lord, and the Spirit is empowering reality, the proclamation needs to be acted upon, manifested and incarnated. It is impossible to speak of the kingdom of God in a convincing way unless we show forth the powers of the kingdom. Paul said that the "kingdom does not consist in words but in power" (1 Cor. 4:20).

Proclamation is a central dimension of the work of the church; the word of God needs to be shared through the words of the church. The story of Jesus Christ and the story of God's covenent with the people of Israel need to be told and retold time and time again. But the church not only announces God's plan of salvation; it is also called to an active role. As a social community, the church must act in history. Its existence must facilitate the wider manifestation of the kingdom in history.

Do we organize competitive activities so that our members cannot participate in the meetings of neighbourhood groups, trade unions, cooperatives, etc.? Do we include in the intercessory prayers of the congregation those dynamics of the human search for justice that also embody God's care for humanity? Even in the internal life of the church, in the celebration of the sacraments, the actions of the church have secular consequences. Baptism and holy communion, a wedding or a funeral service are all religious events; but they address serious human moments of our life, and they have an inevitable impact on the surrounding community.

In a normative sense, the sacramental, inspirational functions of the church cannot be isolated from its total witness to the whole community and the way it will further God's total plan. The baptism of a child reminds the family and the community that the child is called to be a co-worker with God in the shaping of creation and the building of community. The celebration of a wedding is not just the consecration of a family made up of two people; it is a commissioning of the couple to contribute to the life of the whole community from their privileged coming together in mutual love. Every activity of the church should thus be seen in terms of its calling to proclaim the kingdom. It should be seen as an action that helps spread the knowledge of the kingdom; but it should also be seen as manifesting the reality of the kingdom of God. The church is a protagonist of the kingdom. As servant, its work results in signs of love — in healing, in community building, in acts of service. As prophet, the church announces the good news to the poor, denounces the forces that work against the kingdom, and encourages whoever and whatever manifests the kingdom in concrete ways. As priest, the church intercedes for all people. In its worship life it must incorporate the hopes and needs of the surrounding community.

As the community that announces the kingdom, the church becomes the firstfruit of the kingdom and a pre-taste of its final reality; it becomes a sacrament of the kingdom, revealing to the world God's final goal, a sign in itself pointing towards the kingdom. The eucharist is the fullest expression of this dimension of anticipation of the kingdom. Through bread and wine, we anticipate the banquet of the kingdom, the final communion with God, and "we announce the death of the Lord until he comes" (1 Cor. 11:26).

The church is thus called to witness to God's powerful acts in history. It is the bearer of the secret to all history in Christ. Its vocation is to bear Christ, and that is implemented through proclamation. But given the nature of the reality that is proclaimed, this proclamation can take place only through participation, service, intercession, suffering, love that is lived.

As Jesus Christ is the free invasion of love, so the church is sent in the same freedom to witness to that love. The church is the people entrusted with a particular task in the service of the kingdom of God, but it is not the kingdom and it has no monopoly on it. It is not the only agent of the kingdom. We betray the freedom of the kingdom if we insist that all people should be under the authority of the church. We can no longer accept Christendom as a model. That represented an attempt to create a monolithic community subject to the authority of the church. The vocation of the church is to witness to the kingdom in the midst of history, to point towards the King, to make known to the world what has been revealed to it in the life and ministry of Jesus Christ.

The freedom of the church in its mission

We must further affirm that the church is free to select the appropriate means and ways to fulfill its vocation. We can illustrate this freedom of the church by looking at the first Christian community in Jerusalem as described in the Book of Acts.

a) The coming of the Holy Spirit in Acts 2 is a profound communal and personal experience that generated enthusiasm and enabled people to speak in tongues — and to communicate. The reference to speaking in tongues is evidently a reference to the tower of Babel (Gen. 11:1-9). The Holy Spirit is launching the church as a missionary community of reconciliation, symbolically, dramatically and historically. This new community is sent into the whole world to call all of humanity, scattered in Babel as a consequence of its defiance of God, to become, united with Christ, the real and final link between human beings and God.

b) But what happened provoked the comment: "They are drunk." The action of the Spirit gives rise to surprise and scorn. Peter explains: "They are not drunk, it is too early in the morning for that!" And without realizing it, he finds himself preaching! He goes on to explain and interpret, but that interpretation will not be complete until he addresses the people saying: "Repent and be baptized... in the name of Jesus Christ" (Acts 2:38-39).

c) The community was together, having all things in common, caring for one another according to need, manifesting love in all relationships and celebrating the communion (Acts 2:43-47; 4:32-37). The fact of being a community and its very style of life were the mission and "God was adding to the church those who were being saved".

d) Peter and John go to the temple to pray. They see a lame man begging at the door. Love takes hold of the apostles and, before going to pray, they stop to heal. The healing produces amazement, and Peter is obliged to explain what happened. He proclaims Jesus as the Christ and invites people to repent. He acts in freedom and that freedom opens the door to the proclamation of the gospel.

e) Then follows a series of circumstances that lands the apostles in prison. From prison to the temple and back to prison! Confronted with the questioning of the authority (Acts 4:5), they give testimony to the power under which they find themselves and the vocation that is given to them.

They cannot stop giving testimony to Jesus because they must obey God rather than men (4:19-20).

They were clear about their vocation. Their service of the kingdom is to give witness to Jesus Christ. Obliged to explain the events of Pentecost, the healing, the disobedience to authorities, they do so by pointing to the source of their calling. They engage in all kinds of activities, some on their own as they respond in love to a situation and others as they are called to account, through the persecution they face. But all of them become entry points to bear testimony to the total care of God for people and to the calling they have received.

The early church, following the example of Jesus Christ, felt free to respond spontaneously or in organized ways. There was the time when they had to organize a division of labour between the apostles and the deacons (Acts 6:1-7) in order to correct an injustice. What we come across is not anarchy, but it is not a rigid organization either. Stephen is a deacon, but we see him preaching — very soon after the division of labour was made! There must be divisions of labour, but not an oppressive law which would prevent any member of the community from pointing towards the kingdom and inviting others to Jesus Christ.

f) They are all scattered under persecution (Acts 8:1-4). It is not a planned outreach programme, but it provides an opportunity for the disciples to explain why they are where they are and what is happening in Jerusalem. Implicit in that explanation is an evangelistic invitation: this has meaning for you, too, and not only for the people in Jerusalem!

g) Acts could be called the book of the Spirit. We have a series of Spirit surprises: Philip being led to the encounter with the Ethiopian eunuch (Acts 8:26-38); Christ unexpectedly confronting Paul on the road to Damascus (9:1-19); Cornelius and Peter both being led by visions to an encounter (10:1-11:18) which brings home to the church God's missionary concern for the Gentiles. During the first missionary journeys of Paul and Barnabas (13:1-4), time and again the church is surprised by God's calling it to face entirely new missionary situations (10:17; 16:9-10).

Paul is passionately convinced that his vocation is to proclaim the gospel and to get as many as he can to accept the new faith (1 Cor. 9:19-23). But when he is asked not to forget the poor, he gladly takes on the new task. That was the main recommendation made by the Council of Jerusalem, to take care of the poor (Gal. 2:10; 2 Cor. 9). Paul does not hesitate to interrupt his missionary journeys and take to Jerusalem the funds he has collected for the victims of famine (Rom. 15:25-26). In freedom he responds to the challenges which new situations bring up.

The freedom of obedience
Following the example of the early church, the church today is free to make options, to fulfill its missionary calling in the most diverse ways and in the most different circumstances. There is only one priority for the church — to reflect and mediate the love manifested in Jesus Christ. There is only one goal — the kingdom. There is only one central reference — Jesus the King. And there is one concrete, historical concentration point — the poor and the powerless.

A document produced in 1959 by the World Council of Churches refers to this freedom of the church in these terms:

> There is no single way to witness to Jesus Christ. The church has borne witness in different times and places in different ways. This is important. There are occasions when dynamic action in society is called for; there are others when a word must be spoken; others when the way Christian people live together and with others is itself the telling witness. On still other occasions the simple presence of a worshipping community or individual is the witness. These different dimensions of witness to the one Lord are always a matter of concrete obedience. To take them in isolation from one another is to distort the gospel. They are inextricably bound together, and together give the true dimensions of evangelism. The important thing is that God's redeeming word be proclaimed and heard.[1]

---

[1] *A Theological Reflection on the Work of Evangelism*, Geneva, WCC, 1959, p.21.

Of course, we recognize that there are gifts, callings, divisions of labour. Such gifts can be personal or collective. A religious order or a missionary organization working in the inner city or involved in a cross-cultural mission to proclaim the gospel to people who are far away from any Christian church makes its own witness. But we must recognize all such enterprises as contingent answers, actions to be taken here and today and not necessarily to be repeated tomorrow, there or here. The vocations and the contingencies stand in a reciprocal relation of freedom and not of law.

The evangelist who is confronted with a situation of human need cannot argue that his or her gift lies in another direction. We are all called to serve this total invasion of love in the kingdom of God. The division of labour, the recognition of different gifts and the creation of specialized organizations are all necessary, but they should not undermine the freedom which obedience demands or take away from the plenitude of the kingdom of God.

What are the priorities prescribed for the church in our day? Three points of concentration are generally proposed. They arise from God's particular care for the poor, God's sending of the church to proclaim the gospel to all nations, and God's promise of a new day of peace and justice. My thesis is that these are intimately inter-related aspects of one and the same call to Christian obedience in the service of the kingdom, which is basically a call to freedom.

The risks of freedom

This freedom is not something new; it belongs to the being of the church and the service of the kingdom. It has often been manifested in the history of the church, and it is to be manifested today. A rapid selective survey will reveal how such freedom has been exercised, sometimes with positive and at other times negative consequences.

First, even today Orthodox theology would like to preserve a certain harmony between the church and the civil authorities. This is based on the conviction that both are meant to work for the common good of the people and that, working together, they would be a blessing for all people. For us, from a western church perspective, it is reminiscent of the unhappy history of the alliance between church and state which began with Constantine. In our books of history and theology, and even in current discussions of the situation of the church, we often express a certain regret that the Christian church became the official church of the Roman Empire.

But we need to raise the question as to whether the prevailing conditions of the Roman Empire offered any responsible alternative. I am not a church historian, and I can only raise the question. Are we not too quick in condemning a particular event because of the consequences that followed? In this case the consequences were not apparent when the option was made. That option was made so that the witness of the church and the values of the civilization symbolized by the Roman Empire could be preserved. Later the church became a prisoner to the logic of power, and from a persecuted church turned into a persecuting church. That was a tragedy, and it proves that no solution, no one expression of the freedom of the church is final. We must continually ask the question: How do we testify today, anew, to the Servant King of the kingdom of God?

At the present time, in the dynamics of the culture of Eastern Europe, the state seeks to be an entirely autonomous centre of culture and values in terms of Marxist philosophy. The church is making an effort to keep close to the people, to the national history, to the language, affirming as part of its vocation the preservation of that tradition. The most striking example of this is the church in Romania, though the most popular one, as far as the media are concerned, is the Roman Catholic Church in Poland. Where traditionally there had been a close relationship between the church and the state, the church now is no longer involved in the state; instead it comes closer to the people and upholds the national values. The freedom of the church takes account of the factors of power in a given society, and chooses not to be identified with the state. It is related to but also critical of the state; it does not become civil religion, but in freedom follows its vocation.

A second historical example, also polemic in nature, is monasticism. Nothing in Jesus' ministry indicated that this would be a normal phenomenon in the life of the church. The early church did not, as far as we know, commend it as a style of life. Monasticism represented an attempt to preserve the integrity of the Christian faith when there was the possibility that it would be compromised through the alliance of church and state. It was also an attempt to escape from the corrupt world and preserve personal spirituality. But soon, the monasteries developed into centres which offered hospitality to foreigners and refuge to those in need. They developed into hospitals, and later on, into schools and centres of intercessory prayer. From the monasteries came the missionary impulse which led to the conversion of the whole of central and northern Europe. The church had freely assumed an institutional form that already existed in other religious systems. The monastic style of life corresponded to Qumran, to various gnostic sects, even to centres of Hindu spirituality. What began as a retreat, an escape from the world, became transformed into a powerful missionary instrument. The reformers were critical of monasticism; there was no place for it in the churches they founded. They denounced the degradation of the monastic ideal in the sixteenth century. Once again we find that we cannot absolutize any instrumentality that the church has made use of in the past, in responsibility and freedom, to cope with a particular need at a historical moment. Nor can we dismiss such movements; they are all possible methodologies in the work of the church.

Let us look at two contemporary models of concentration adopted on the basis of perceived priorities. One is the concentration on church growth as the main goal of Christian mission, in terms of cross-cultural evangelism and of planting and developing numerically growing churches. This has always been a priority for the church.

During the last two centuries this has been the dominant model of western mission. From a kingdom perspective it cannot be challenged. We need to fulfill the Great Commission. We must reveal God's purpose to the whole of humankind and in all cultures. We need to call people to become co-workers, participants, in the active, historical struggles of the kingdom of God. But if it becomes an end in itself, and church growth does not obtain within a concern for the totality of the kingdom, it becomes irresponsible. Church growth, when it degenerates into mere recruitment of members to a club, becomes a betrayal of the kingdom. But the possibility of abuse is not an excuse to evade the missionary challenge that it contains.

The other example has to do with the present concern for Christian participation in liberation struggles. We could use the example of Nicaragua or South Africa, or the priority for mission which Desmond Tutu recommends for the churches in that region. We cannot evade the call to witness to God's saving and liberating news. If the church of Jesus Christ does not tackle the question of the oppression of millions of people, especially the question of racism as institutionalized and practised in South Africa, the whole credibility of the gospel will suffer. So this particular vocation is a privileged one, absolutely necessary, if we want to proclaim in a convincing manner the message of the kingdom. But if this same emphasis on Christian participation in liberation struggles does not include the dimensions of celebration and worship, and of discerning the eschatological pointers to the kingdom that is coming and the Christ who is King, then that too becomes a betrayal of the gospel.

The fact that in the struggle for liberation in Latin America people are taking time to develop a theology, is itself an indication of their awareness that they are not in a "secular struggle", but that the shaping of new societies is a matter of Christian obedience, and an important means of proclaiming the gospel.

Gustavo Gutierrez said:

> In Jesus Christ we encounter God. In the human word we read God's word. In the historical events, we recognize the fulfilment of the promise. This is the hermeneutical fundamental circle: from human being to God and from God to human being, from history to faith and from faith to history, from fraternal love to the love of the Father and from the love of the Father to the love of the brothers and sisters, from the human justice to the holiness of God and from the holiness of God to

the human justice, from the poor to God and from God to the poor.[2]

There is no guarantee that missionary freedom will not be misused. In the ecumenical dialogue we have the possibility of continually challenging, correcting and inspiring one another.

But are there not axioms or "logical" priorities in mission? We need to face this question. The consultation on evangelism and social responsibility held in June 1982 in Grand Rapids, Michigan, stated that the two concerns of justice and evangelism belong intimately together, and while they can be distinguished, they cannot and should not be separated. The participants affirmed, however:

> Evangelism relates to people's eternal destiny; in bringing them the good news of salvation, Christians are doing what nobody else can do. Seldom, if ever, should we have to choose between satisfying spiritual and physical hunger, or between helping bodies and saving souls. An authentic love for our neighbour will lead us to serve him or her as a whole person. Nevertheless, if we must choose, then we have to say that the supreme and ultimate need of all humankind is the saving grace of Jesus Christ, and that therefore a person's eternal and spiritual salvation is of greater importance than his or her temporal and material wellbeing.[3]

There are others who feel that priority should be given to acts of mercy; they do not want to proclaim the gospel in words, and they are even willing to suppress their very identity as Christians. In the sixties, in Europe, a theology of Christian presence in the world was developed which went to the extreme of demanding total silence on the part of Christians. It prescribed a moratorium on words in order first to earn the right to be heard. But it cannot be a permanent solution or recommendation, for there is a story to be told.

---

[2] *La fuerza historica de los pobres*, Salamanca, Sigueme, 1982, p.81 (my translation).
[3] *Evangelism and Social Responsibility*, Exeter, Paternoster Press, 1982, pp.24-25.

We must say no to any attempt to permanently prioritize the ways and means of obedience in the service of the kingdom. The only priority is the kingdom, the King and his invasion of love. And the word spoken and a glass of cold water given in Jesus' name are both, depending on the circumstances, correct entry points into the total dynamic of the kingdom. There can be no gospel of individual salvation without reference to the justice of the kingdom. There is no love of God unrelated to my neighbour. The encounter between church members and persons outside the Christian community is, *de facto*, a total encounter where words receive meaning from the entire behaviour of the Christian community. We cannot decide whether our neighbour is saved; that *needs* to wait for the final surprise of the Last Judgment (Matt. 7:21-23, 25:31-46). We proclaim salvation *in* Christ. That means salvation in his body, salvation in his kingdom, salvation in his plan to transform all reality. So any word that announces the gospel is an entry point into the total kingdom; if not it is not an authentic proclamation of the gospel. And no Christian solidarity with the poor can exist which does not point to the totality of the kingdom promises including the invitation to personal faith and witness. To quote Gustavo Gutierrez once again:

> The liberating praxis, inasmuch as it is part of an authentic solidarity with the poor and oppressed, is finally a praxis of love, of real love, efficient, historical love for concrete people, love to the neighbour, and in that love, love to Christ who identified himself with the least of our brethren. All attempts to separate love of God and neighbour give place to attitudes that make the gospel poorer. It is easy to oppose a praxis of heaven to a praxis of earth and vice versa. It is easy, but it is not faithful to a gospel of God-made-man. It seems more authentic and more profound to talk of a praxis of love that has its roots in a free, gratuitous love of the Father as it becomes history in solidarity with the poor and dispossessed, and through them, in solidarity with all human beings.[4]

There is, after Jesus Christ, such an incarnation of God in human beings that our roots in Christ bring us to love our

---

[4]*Op. cit.*, p.69 (my translation).

neighbour, and our love of our neighbour brings us to Jesus Christ.

Sent free

The kingdom of God is an eternal reality in God; it is the historical manifestation of God's Trinitarian love. God is in command; he speaks; he preserves; he purifies; he judges; he completes. He will gather up our tentative, partial, ambiguous expressions of obedience. Because we trust in God and believe in God's plan for us today and in eternity, and we pray "Your kingdom come"; because we look to the future with expectation and eagerness; we can, in faith, offer a cup of water, a word of love, the open hand of communion, all in God's name. Preaching the word, interceding in prayer, living in solidarity with the poor — these are all ways to affirm and fulfill our vocation as the church. As a priestly people fulfilling our vocation, we obey our calling by pointing to Jesus the King in whose life every life can find a new beginning.

The biblical model for the vocation of the church is provided by John the Baptist who points to Jesus Christ: "Behold the lamb of God, who takes away the sin of the world." The mission of the church is to point to him through whose life, death and resurrection has been revealed the fullness of God's forgiving and redeeming love. We are haunted by the example of Mary, the mother of Jesus. At the wedding in Cana, she instructs the servants: "Do whatever he tells you." Mary has become a source of inspiration in both Roman Catholic and Orthodox piety; she can also be such for Protestants. She calls our attention to him, on whose authority alone we can rely.

Paul, on the road to Damascus, is given the vision of the risen Christ. His response gives us the final paradigm for the mission of the church. "What shall I do, Lord?" (Acts 22:10). Missionary freedom means asking Christ what we shall do, and being perpetually prepared to do what he asks of us.